THIS CONSTELLATION
IS A NAME

Collected Poems 1965-2010

ALSO BY MICHAEL HELLER

POETRY

Two Poems

Accidental Center

Knowledge

Figures Of Speaking

In The Builded Place

Marginalia In A Desperate Hand

Wordflow

Exigent Futures: New And Selected Poems

A Look At The Door With The Hinges Off

Eschaton

Beckmann Variations & other poems

PROSE

Living Root: A Memoir

Earth And Cave

Two Novellas: Marble Snows & The Study

ESSAYS

Conviction's Net Of Branches: Essays On The Objectivist Poets And Poetry

Uncertain Poetries: Essays On Poets, Poetry And Poetics

Speaking The Estranged: Essays On The Work Of George Oppen

EDITOR

Carl Rakosi: Man And Poet

Poets Poems #21

THIS CONSTELLATION
IS A NAME

Collected Poems 1965-2010

Michael Heller

MICHAEL HELLER

11 May 2012

For Mark,
All best wishes,

Nightboat Books
Callicoon, New York

This Constellation Is A Name: Collected Poems 1965 - 2010
© 2012 by Michael Heller
Printed in the United States

ISBN: 978-1-937658-02-1

Cover art: Charles Burchfield, *Orion in December,* 1959.
Smithsonian American Art Museum, Gift of S.C. Johnson & Son, Inc.
Reproduced with permission of Charles E. Burchfield Foundation.

Design and typesetting by HR Hegnauer
Text set in Constantia

Cataloging-in-publication data is available
   from the Library of Congress

Distributed by University Press of New England
One Court Street
Lebanon, NH 03766
www.upne.com

Nightboat Books
Callicoon, New York
www.nightboat.org

CONTENTS

KNOWLEDGE (1979)

BECKMANN VARIATIONS AND OTHER
POEMS (2 0 1 0)

Beckmann Variations

In memory of my parents, Martha and Peter Heller,
and for Jane, my son Nick and my sister Tena,
and in gratitude to friends

A LOOK AT THE DOOR
WITH THE HINGES OFF

(2006)

Poems from the mid-1960s

7 PRAISES

Be drunk.
Be the body
drunk. Drunk.

Move to become;
be
ruffled.

Wind become.
Be as
brought here.

Be loosed.
Be kept.
Be loosed. Lost.

Wind you are;
know it.
Be light.

Find light.
Be found
as in it.

Be,
as being is.
Be born.

OK EVERYBODY, LET'S DO THE MONDRIAN STOMP

small red block
beside a long
white block

tall white
block beside
a large

white block
yellow block
under the

tall white block
then a small
white block

and a long
white block
and a

blue block
locked
in a corner

TO MY AUTO HORN

Be beep

preserve
my
radiance

HERE IN THIS ROOM

Here in this room I giggle
and feel a glass thorn
sticking in my throat
I don't laugh too hard;
it quivers, and I am reassured
by its tickle.

Here in this room
there is a brass horn, but I
do not play it.
In this room the horn
itself is best
Any sound it would make
simple muffled vibrations of its swollen air.

Here in this room
I am the victim of received impressions,
so that a cry
I might make
is the personal voice
against which the wall
wears thought like a badge.

Here in this room
my sadness sighs
below minimum voltage
and a generator hums
into the hammered air.

L U L U

i.m. Hannah Weiner d. 1997

1

what oh where oh what . . .
the earth or you
asleep in the quiet peace
of yourself
and night, why not night
you won't allow
its stars and blackness
it was the same with January
an edict after New Year's Eve
for once sober, mindful of the traffic
along the unsafe wet streets
everyone tooling into morning
with hangovers and resolutions
later the card game broke up
(I still had my pants on
you were down to your undies)
Alphonso told us quite candidly about
the history of Spain
and as if that weren't enough
we wondered about the color of the hibiscus
(was it pink, or rouge, or rose-red) such
nit-picking
in the morning

gracious hostess with henna hair
and rhinestone studded shoes
you speak with fork'd tongue
about the "100 Greatest Books"
and I, who have studied my every flaw
in the mirror ask how
you love me (though I preferred
you) and was being devious
it was then that things took a turn
attitudes, poses, all our clever regalia
and you, Most Gracious Hostess
you, from the *sancta sanctorum* of your bridge set
said:
go, go and get me ice
FADE OUT AND LOUIS CAPET
and her kitchen very menacing

3

in *la finestrina, il sole, il sole*
it was hot, we liked apples
even simple

4

O ____! O sweet ____! Name of names
____!
____! I say again. You forgot
nothing, not even the anniversary of
October, the year's dullest month
and rightly so
it was too cold (it's always too cold)
to plunge into the stream
and yet we have to kiss her

5

here is a plaster wall
step up to it or turn your back
on its indifferent whiteness
(it is the same)
(it is the same)

6

at last

sunlight

leaves

wispy gowns

you wore

by windows

bedding

moon's rise

night wall

slips

loves all

up and

down

7

"in the beginning" you said
there were "all endings"
and "in all endings"
there was, at least
hope

APRIL POEM

1

Out where the sea
went to sleep nodding
at porpoises and risings and settings of the sun

I dreamed an eight-foot dream
it was green and had carbuncles
and an old aunt sat in it
chewing radishes.

2

The enigma of the party—
until the parakeet's release
and joined our other friends.

3

O magic fireplug
the curbside serenade's the most
With the moon
we found puddles of ice.

PLANETS

that their orbits are elliptic

or like the old

proved not for a center

one can live without
vanity of invention and yet

find disbelief or not

the trend boys . . . is anonymity

to be safe if
it is assumed

not to exist
and leaves
enough to cover everyone

AFTERTHOUGHT

many things recurring

skies, suns, stammering
anew each day

my blare

is the blare of the end of the week

but I ignore its radio silence

I have jobs, have had jobs
never could work

now and then I put my pencil down
beside a natural quiet

that lets what passes pass

WEATHER EYE

1

by the eye

by space that falls across the eye

tufts of twig
and branch wavering

all things written
in their own lines

perhaps we, one day . . .

     a resembling

the rhymes of many things

      . . . convinced of a common

clarity

before it rains

2

as in an impossible procedure

the volume of the weeks and years

scribbles of lines
down that rich black slope

not my life in words
but words in my life

you see
this matters

        dance against dance

in the storm head: pre-figurations

3

across that sky

the figures of a graceful language

my love, my speech . . .

abhors itself   its knowledge

a potential rain the

wind disperses

                   love

not simple enough
to say

a dance, there,
beyond an eye or an ear of that wind

was to occur within you

now
it pulls the words away

no spaces

the curious mixtures

invisible yards and yards of
everything

as on a blank page, named. . .

the curtains spotted

with remembered rain

A I R

1

who sound loves
needs a plunge

beneficent duke out
around his fief
caught poachers at it

                      we were out of line
                      here and there
                      and sang so

2

indeed   hung up
we missed you
asked where you'd gone

. . . spread
everywhere

3

glad we met
you
he told the guest
who stayed

4

the May never came

the ample woman asked
about

you going and going
at once

FRAGMENT

the hidden harmony is better—Heraclitus

laughed

                    thought of the coins
                    beside

the wrinkled Kleenex

                            is the shoe?

how 'this age'
         will bear it   to be
                              excluded   the hand
against
your knowledge: her
secrets, what

she looked like   your eye

says everyone at once

excludes design of
spontaneity   and that

before us stretch

the young girls'

                    neither firm
                    nor soft

perfection

POEM SEQUENCE

1

Day eyes
dissembling trees

comes to me—
presence of weights

2

Yes
held to
as to hold
or to let go

Desire is
your nose

is the aroma of
something sightful

3

Absence of light
calculating presence

Be

Be as one displaced
by the lesson of light

4

Avoid the map

"a heaviness moves thee"

5
  (fragments, shards)

. . . the cow might see . . .
. . . the wind might scrape . . .

. . . believe in that
  finitude
  at least . . .

. . . the light/drunk
  moves
  through fields . . .

6

See: tree
    & tree's shadow:

    the two-pronged
    blossom
    of the same plant

7

Trees
dissembling day eyes

comes of presence
weighs me

FOCAL PLANE

an urgent

abstraction, the limit of

concretion/eye

is art　　　　more so

the human　　scales the world, the

successive

reminiscences of a thing's

properties

ONE ON THE MUSE

Once, there were eyes, then ears . . .

The age existed, exists; it streams continually
out of a disfigured mouth

And where you are going or have been,
the words erode

the continuity you call
yourself

Now, how differently
you will wear your pants

and stand multiplied in the garden in a
new sun's light—

After you've examined the flowers
will all of you then

go home

ET CETERA

those birds gone   other things

that were a line of flight across your mind

the fact was

                                    you were

to be told less

never mind the sun up

and the banner that morning
become your thoughts

the night before
the concerted darkness asked for messages

and out of a boiling sea
you rose
dragging birds and all
(e.g. sea-weed, crabs and fishes)

today,
as if to underscore your loss

there is a loud roar with each wave

and far off, a rather constant waving

5 TH H A R M O N I C

the month
looks through its grey prism
like a mallet

its tired eyes
stretch and stretch

over newly
polished floors

there is also more room here
than rain

or hands
tapping

or even new
mailboxes

to reel about
endless wondering
how the walls work

A LOOK AT THE DOOR WITH
THE HINGES OFF

1

In white suits, on a white-washed terrace, Pound and Fenollosa sat at a
white painted wrought iron table with a glass top, drinking a milky white
drink, ouzo perhaps or a mixture of milk and water. At that time, Fenollosa
had grown a rather large black moustache which stood out against the
whiteness of the scene like one of his inimitable Chinese characters.

2

In white suits, pagination permitted, the terrace washed in white paint,
a light rain had fallen, which now the heat of the sun, pulsating behind
the clouds, changed to steam. Ouzo was brought out by the waitress, a
young girl with very white skin whose dark eyes hung in the white space
of the scene like two dots in the negative of a photograph taken through a
telescope trained on Sirius and Canis.

3

In control of the whites, Franz Kline claimed he was not a calligrapher,
painting the white portions of his later canvases with as much concern as
he showed for the blacks. Canis and Fenollosa would have gotten along
well together.

4

We have a problem with white. It is the grace of saying it. Something we
like—a flash of color, an absolute aimlessness to our intensity—the world
will suffer less.

5

At every point a node of energy clung to the white wool of her dress. It was all very sexy.

6

The grand themes demand a certain silence, a sense of quietude which precludes pompous utterance. Here, my dearest, the ubiquity of the world in clean white sheets.

EARTH AND CAVE

(2006)

Poems from 1966

White plumed reeds

above yerba buena

—a clear dry smell

but the fact of nature

so complexly given

I was no more of it

than you, a swift

mindless carrier beyond,

beyond that one

so perfectly real

in wanting, and

no thought then

seemed deeper

White plumed

sea reeds

a tassel

a keepsake

of no wisdom

SHORT TAKES ON THE BUS

woman carries
wide basket
cloth cover dancing
over baby chicks

a shepherd
sleeps off a drunk
low grumble of a snore
smelling of goats—
his friends
have to lead him off the bus
—might as well be a goat!

sting of fresh laid manure in nostrils
too hot to close windows
suffocate or smell shit—reminds me of a joke
but really wish I had a cold

from Málaga to Granada over mountains
going full tilt around curves
no guard rails/wondering how to sit
so all bones won't be broken if we go over—
even the locals are yelling at the driver to slow down
but he points at boxed-in face of Jesus over seat
steps on gas and laughs
I can't take it/move to seat
away from window

wanting so badly to piss
ready to jump out
at next town

dead of night
the bus
tunnels in its own lights
carrying all motion/direction

people getting on   off
many stops
in the middle of nowhere

SUNDAY/SUNDOWN

Candy papers
blow
from the Paseo

    into sea
        into sea
you want so much
to know

names garland everything
words stacked, tiered to flesh

the parities
forever rising

—love's
dark sense—

a sea banded
over orange light
dims cross half horizon

plethora
moods swim up to

plethora
of tensed shape
of elaborate occurrence

vivid as colored papers afloat
the emulations of wave motions

the passions we ride on
being in, making love
adorn our bodies

I have found my force in you
half-light, half-dark arcings
of pleasure and silence—

so much done together
natural, cloven
yet joined

audacious desire
have you writhe under me
come so sweetly

Kops's
kids
play with their Spanish friends
—together they kill a bird
with stones

then Kops's kids
run home
crying over what they have done
—the village kids
put the dead bird in an old cigar box
sing *Aves*
bury it
and cry for the bird

A POLITICAL POEM

Good day.

The air so clear it singes.

We have our own clarity to meet.
Painted white, the walls and stairways, painted white
which are encountered—
for that is what it is
Never so much *not* a mere presence
as when the ground, not hard
but durable
is under
the feet

Whose village is this?

Beneath the eaves of the *Alcalde's* house
are the abandoned nests
of the African stork
which by some erratic synapse
flocks to the town every four or five years
on its way north

Plunging deep—
about 30 feet—
the blackish green bulk of the dead sea turtle
spins on edge like a coin
in the rip of the current
And the month before we left
a dead dolphin—that sign of luck!
The *niños* playing heroes tied a rope to its tail
and pulled it up the beach

The rich and the poor alike live
in a profusion of flowers
No spring, no season
The geranium, the bougainvillea are always there
And the not-so-rich and the just-rich
tend also the plastic flower

If we wonder
why we waste our time
If we find that we can still wonder . . .

The old men do not matter
The old men whose voices croak
their *buenos dias*
eyes away
shuffling down the path
to crap behind the rocks

BEFORE BREAKFAST

walk downstairs
stepping only where sun
has warmed the tiles

grind coffee

Go out for bread
white walls
black doorways
black crook of
a woman

the baker's face
white as a Kabuki dancer's

slap, slap of his mechanical
kneader

juggle home the hot loaf

nearly dropping it
passing the cascade of bougainvillea
on fire
      where the sun passes through

FISHERMEN'S QUARTER

now
they are again
home

in otherwise
unlit streets
before each house
a small fire

BURIANA BEACH

the tall weeds
weathered white
a screen behind the horse
nuzzling at grass fringe
on which the field hand put son
and the horse stepped
dignified up and down the beach

past the German girl in bikini
whose sex   later
bare backed he must have felt
—astride him
her beauty was unmistakable
and when the horse reared, the very image of mounting,
as she on him—
forelegs and cock
flailing air—
this
          she held to

*

sun up
the keels of the boats up
the men sleep under
eyes and cockpits
of those open boats
turned from sky—a blue
one cannot know
and not return to
—so easily tossed
in sea

"I was told hardly any
learn to swim, they go out too far . . . night
 . . . anguish . . .
to try
to make it back"

the old men
the survivors
they come to live in daylight
mending nets

or older
sitting quietly on the *Paseo*
shielding their eyes
from the sun   or what?

FISHING

for Hugh

Look deep.

We are not ourselves
But the paradox, we are no other.

Thoreau said: "the places that have known me,
they are lost." For he knew none,
Not Walden nor the storm-swept Cape
in anyway useful to him.
I mean he kept going back.
He had to go back.
I mean here we are
and it isn't enough.

*

First thing
a rowboat is brought up
and anchored just past the surf
while men on shore carefully fold the net.
Then the boat is beached
and the net put in.
A line from one end of it
is tied to a rock on shore,
and the boat is launched
to make a mile-wide sweep of the bay,
the men in the boat paying out the net
as she goes
till finally they return to shore
about a hundred yards down the beach
with the other end of the net.

Again the boat is anchored offshore,
and the men group themselves at either end
of the net lines
and begin hauling it in,
using a short length of rope to which a rock is knotted
which they hurl around the net lines, then turn,
pulling from over their shoulders,
faces red, neck, thigh and back muscles straining
while the youngest kids
make a game of laying the wet lines on the sand
in perfect circles.

—the beggar—
syphilis has eaten away his nose
maybe his brain/he
stands before you
neither proud
nor ashamed
with his hand out

he is not his ugliness

Find sense to change?

The mountains did, every day, the sun shifting
in declination

Leap

The actual stumped them. The dark
did nothing
but remind them of their own dark

root like
          impacted
gripping down
for warmth, water
          or what—
ever was up that gorge
the *grandee* walked out of
a string of rabbits
slung on his servant's arm

My wife jumped

Black
we'd never
known
          "Living nights"
we called them

that whistle
in high woods
above
river bed
following us for miles

until the rocks
seized us

—the two
cliffs
face to face
the way no one
could be
with any of them
and not draw up one's own terror
—cold
as the quick cold
torrent
of water
swirling
over our feet
we tried to shout above
for some nameless
quality of contact

DREAM

And the rain clouds ripped loose from the deeply colored peaks of the
Sierra Morenos. *All you wanted then*. As if your nature were a parched
lip and the soft tendrils of cloud your oasis. For under all this, under this
sky of turbulence and unfulfilled promise, the countryside lay which in
honesty you did not belong to. And the rain was a symbol, in that both of
you desired to receive it.

This fact pierced me with sudden aloneness. I had no words, even for my
wife. That is, I remember leaving the house day after day. To walk in the
fields. *You walked in the fields*. You were a curiosity. To the fieldhands,
to the beetles with their bright enameled backs. Stopping to let the
attentions wander. An absurd elusive sense of self all the more alive
because what seemed to slip away was just that attention, the holding of
which was proof, at least in words, of the term "alive."

The beetles; since everything was of equal importance. I mean none of it
was unimportant. The grass alive with them crawling obliviously over my
shoe. The pure perfect life of the beetle, which sickened me. The beetle
which might drown in the symbolical rain. If it rained. For the dream
could not undercut the geography.

ACCIDENTAL CENTER

(1972)

in the difficulties of the rough seas
of the passage—for that
is what it was—a thing to be endured,
but for the beauty of the powerful lunges
of the dolphins seen
from the deck a wildness
in the seas, as wild as seas and
natural, as we knew
ourselves not
in the blindered shuttered salon
as the heart jumped
when the rose
and its fluted vase
fell to the table
after an untoward roll

                     —untoward as the steel meaning
unbending of the ship's prow
or the rock's entrapment
against which, a wild sea
and wild dolphins . . .

                  kinship

and miscalculation

PRESSURE:

Didn't you say you loved me?

under what conditions

under what
under what
under what

_____

under the air
@ 15 lbs per square inch on the roof
on the safety-factored I-beams
                                slipping down through curtain walls
to the ground
to gravitational bedrock
                        accidental center: home

            *

which we sailed from

under black
and glitter

irony
and smugness
facing out on the frozen rocks
of the universe

the hard energy

spectral pinpricks

excitations given and received

the pulsar's wave peak
falling from enormous source
on the steel mesh of the antenna
drowning the signal of the probe
impaled on the far-off planet

whim and fantasy and power

                    *

the radio at sea
the monstrous groans of the empty airwaves
for two days
midpoint Atlantic

now
to face ourselves
amid the gush of plumbing
the whirr of ventilators packing air into the cabin

                    *

My God
        what we felt
one night on the deck
of the NOVI
             the beat of engines
through her plates
                     overhead
the tenuous milk clouds

their silent movements

myriad possibilities

concrete and eternal

spaced as waves

feel THIS
            she said, wanting desperately my participation

awash in the bombarding cosmic rays
in the mysterious cosmos
itself on the heights
                 of cause and being

THE CARDIAC POEM

1

Blaiberg's heart,

a way to keep modern?

The thought fierce. Little trip
hammer of a beat
to plow a body
thru that much more
time and space

at first there was a wobble
a neutral, a scientific
wobble

simply a matter of fit

2

and later
they make it fit—

O imagine
the recessional

as if time
leapt back

the way sun is seen

at 6:00 PM
—a great red ball

and a minute later
on the world's rim
distended by the thick waves of air

the way we must seem
from the point of view
of the sun

and at 7:00
all is dark

3

the aura I have made round you
meaning
you are *its* heart, its center

is more than fleshing out

is beauty
the way frost coats
a tree

to the finest tendrils
of its branchings

O the delicacy
of the image

Though neither you
nor I
are fragile

the frost is—
it snaps
or is defrosted at the end of a cycle

4

And in dream
Barnard, white coat and stethoscope
an Aztec priest

but a thief
stealing what belongs to the Sun
secreting it
in the open swimming cavity

after the stitches
after the wipe-up
after the groggy headache of anesthesia

someone would realize
in what way
it had been offered up

5

Via Cain or via Abel

in what way
if it happened
it could kill you

just hearing
thump
silence
thump
at night

the panic of love
and not love
twisted
round you

6

shaky heart

bird

its salt pulse: song
that keeps one alive

I love you. That
I Ching of possibility
which has been grasped
then pulled beyond me

till it is no longer me

nor you

7

a flutter
a seizure; thick
fibers that contract

a bird
crushed in a cage
of tissue and fluids—the heart sac

how many medieval men
saw the heart?

how many
see the unneutral
heart of Arts and Letters

8

at what end of what thing
do the names of the Gods change
from ennui of loneliness

There isn't anything we can't do
now
not one thing

a wall is a wall
and what of a wall

Have you ever seen them
harvest wheat? The scythe
death of wheat?

THE BODY: A FABLE

meeting you
    ·   or meeting anyone
I am sick
with my own
clumsiness

the clumsiness Nietzsche
cried against
tending that corpse all night
      —his fallen brother—
who he set in the hollow of a tree
that wolves not savage it

and at dawn
Nietzsche woke
and left the dead
shedding artifice after artifice
as he walked from the woods
to be wolfish then among men
roaming their darkness . . .

yet each night dreaming
of him in the log
—by now sheer putrescence
seeping to the roots

and was glad so natural a thing
became man
      though likewise, it
filled him
with terror . . .

so the dream went

*

and though free of the forest
each morning Nietzsche woke and despaired
how stubbed in that dream his arms had become
how thick the neck and bent low
by him who he carried
boned in his chest, thinking
this must be the world on my back
but it is only my dead brother

and which hung in him
awkward and pained
dumb and stupid
with anyone

this despite the glad
thing he had seen its death to be

he who had put himself
away from wolves
where now fear held him

wanting to speak to and embrace
whom he met
from the body that was his
not the one
yet to bury

TAURUS POEM

*

sometimes I am beside a woman
who holds my life

I stand in the dark
over the soft curve of her back

and want to touch it

*

three years straining weights
latissimus dorsi
called them `lats', `bat's wings'

in pain and fury
screaming out
punching the barbell murderously at the ceiling

outer tissue ruptured
a soreness
as muscle rebuilt itself
harder, thicker

impacting anger

wanting to make myself attractive to women
and stronger

*

that madness
locked there now. don't ever
touch. between my shoulder blades

bands of bunched humiliation. in Spain
when I saw the sword
enter the bull's hump
I relaxed

watched his harassed death
abstractly

focusing
on the rhythmic jets
of blood from his nostrils

why do I think
of my cock
emptying in you

I want to die fucking you
and almost do

*

once a bull chased me
up a road

in Peekskill. I was
seven years old. the next day
fenced in the pasture
he stood patiently
by the boards
as I jeered:

'die, die, die'

*

cap-pistol wars

later a crowd
and field shrunk
to the ribbing of a thigh pad

to the bone grunt of hip
thrown at his middle

and past the eyes
banks of light
jet and skimmer

and both go down

a point reached
at which
you are just inside your skin

what are you doing?

*

china shop life

I set my head between shoulders: bull dog
an All-American stance
goring the Green Bay Packer
thru a film of red
the Asian's unpadded belly
look and smell of his entrails
driving me wild

America: you Brahma and rodeo
roped together

I remember mounting her from behind
blind rage
kicking down the slats of my body

*

he put his horn into the *barrio* and flipped a plank
across the sand, his unsureness
became his madness
sweet to let those juices flow
'we are at the beginning of a radical depopulation

                                                    of the earth'

we've buggered the world
with our impossible anger

hunched over you
I just don't know
if I love or hate

THE PORTRAIT

in the silvered depths
the figure

in continuous time
the fact of image
flung in photons
into the moment

and fixed

a danger
apparent danger

there in the emulsion
is the figure

at its back
a wall
and on the wall
its shadow
bending deeper
into the film

some other
at some other labor

bearing the burden
of its darkness
and its death

that the forward
looking face
might rise from

OPERATION CICERO

writing of the great light of cities

and would hope these things might be changed
by the power of an idiom

as in the film
the spy switches
the bulb
to photograph the secret plans

as the words
all go toward the sight
of secrets

though these are entropic times
and those bright clusters
in our lives

in their rot
are black bodies

and absorb it all, absorb it all
like a woman
on one's bed

who cannot bear the light

THREE BAR REFLECTIONS
ON JOHN COLTRANE

The language of New York has changed a bar and
                                        restaurant
scene to two women talking of lovers black and white,
liberal lovers. She says she saw a man on the street
roughly of his features and mistook the man for him but
that the man was not his color. She says to her friend,
she is color blind, she says she knows all about him.

*

He: a hunched back and boiling red face; beside she: small
and shriveled. Both in the booth, their ugliness uglier
for their awareness. This couple getting thru the world.
A fact imaging a deeper fact. As with only the weight
of notes the song is dragged down thereby amid detritus
and effluvia. Against the sweetness of creation attitudes
are posed because *it* drives back to the core thru all
the secret lives dreamt of, rancorous and jealous of
what is incomplete or unfulfilled overwhelming the music
unless love saves it.

*

History is a joke. Personal history: unfunny.
Knowing everyone to be serious when sick and banging
on the bed for some stranger, but that he should be
like ourselves. And come get drunk or delirious, falling
into someone resembles us. On this, the heart realizes
itself meaningless—its words have moved off beyond
their meanings, as in the music, the whorls of sound
are an eternal trope—an eternal equivalency. Not to be
admitted to my world—I come to his.

MEDITATION ON THE CORAL

1

suppose I should look
down there
for a woman

yet find nothing
more intimate than murder

or bored children playing
a game of hopscotch in the streets

or in the heat,
the close-packed buildings, blurred
and shimmering

waiting with my fellow citizens
for the rain which summer brings
running down the skin

its coolness
comes in time
time to stave off disaster

and its taste
commingled with my own salt
older than any word on my tongue

2

she brought me
a piece of coral

I placed it on the desk
I examined
the wondrous bleached ribbings

the delicate housings
of millespores

I imagined the sea,
its enveloping wetness . . .

3

throughout time
these aggregates

clusters of protozoa
in the primal slime

cells having multiplied
beyond calculation
secrete the porous calc

the hardened branchings and flowerings
that surround them

and there too, new dwellers
have come and gone

swish swash
the sea sounds over them

holding and nourishing

4

breeding
feeding
mutating
survivals

threads visible
and invisible
that form a web

the many tied to one
—that singular complex
which is the secret of the sea

so it is the oldest time
I speak of

and all that touches us
up from that phylum, eons as of
the leaves of trees
for centuries
falling to the earth

the billions of shapes the waves
have taken

all of which has touched us
—to try and touch it back—

yet, to be precise
we've lost that way
and what is left us
is the taste for salt on one's food
or a tepid bath some four flights up

5

and the hierarchies
of hungers
have been reordered

and that is how things are
not just a pessimism of the self
but a terror of each other

and the warm saline
—as of the birth sac
still a dream

some thought of
fluid which still lingers

but from all that has been feared
and suffered, all that we have done
to each other, one comes
to want no more

no more
than more of oneself

and seeks there
for reasons of
what has transpired

so that
the true means of *Okeanos*
may again lead outward from the skin

6

she gave me a piece of coral
it was snow-white
antique white

the white of cities
it is said the antique Venus ruled

the coral, the harmony
of its construction
an after-image of primitive life

and beyond that time
living perhaps beyond the love of it
certainly beyond the love of many

we are together on these shores
breaking and drowning in the surf
of these cities

with an ache for water

MARO SPRING

1

in a tissue
of dusty air

over dry
impoverished fields

no plow
can break

rock pitted
fields

on which
crops of men
have had their backs broken

we pick
ourselves across

crablike
under the sun

2

the cities
the desolations of war

fought for women or fine goods
are human if unreasonable

but this stone
set in stone

—accursed—
until

a mile
into its center

an aureole
of rank vegetation

around
an immense

reverberating
recess

3

he who has come to drink
and goes as we come
is my brother

in our human need

4

I was not thirsty

but craned
my head

past the wet
stones, the world

of elaborate detail
and imagery—

what thunder

into darkness I looked

into darkness I looked
and was happily blind

DOWNTOWN AFTER THE GALLERIES

for Verna & Brad Graves

Bradley's Bar
after Gorky's eye. Walking
from the subway in the slush
then this
warm brown paneled wood
this few
people, instants, to fall into
this clinging . . .

with its mirror above the bar
below which people sit and drink
looking up into the glass
staring down each other
. . .

Gorky's eye: the orbit dark
which looks out
into the world—this eye
of all, chosen to see from
. . .

Before the long sheets of plate glass
give back reflections
a coating of silver .001 inch thick is applied
The coating adds no appreciable strength
to the glass
. . .

The world
thinner than a fingernail in the mirror,

but have you ever
tried to grab through glass?
. . .

In a glance, judged and judging
with only the strength
of a glance: the power
of a beacon
on a rocky coast
or a killer's flashlight
in a dark room

. . .

What reality he had hold of
was not enough
To move from one way of seeing the world
to another
incurs risk
What suffices for me,
not necessarily enough for him

In the changing work,
a distinct sound of
breaking glass

. . .

Some feed thru the face
Some feed on the face
Some feed on the broken, the split—
open face

Some are not fed at all

. . .

Sometimes
it is watching a mirror—
one's own reflection—
smash to the floor

. . .

He wrote, "all the things I haven't got
are God to me"

. . .

It is our look
It is our concern
The iron of the Other in the silvered glass
To be unable to move
To have to remain
To hope to be transfixed
There are ten panels in the mirror
Different people in different panels
They edge nervously one to the next
There are segments in the armor
of man. At each one
love may have stopped
The energy flows from head to pelvis and
"love shines in her . . ."

. . .

Gorky's eye, the one shaded dark
facing out of the drawing
trembling, vulnerable . . .

. . .

Outside it is snowing
I drink down my scotch
savoring its smoky taste
not wanting to go by myself
I scan the mirror
Neither love nor hate are seen
Only a savage need
Only my face

The street dark
at my back
The thinking
how lonely an eye
gets wanting
a loved thing to see
and seeing nothing
himself or itself

4:21 P.M. ON ST. GEORGE'S CLOCK: FILM

for Karen

solitary park
solitary benchers

still air, still branches

the green footage stopped
—matter, call it matter
perceived as light, corpuscles of light
in the "little hole
in the eye . . ."

Delaunay, the painter, prepared
his materials in a darkened room

then
drilled a pinhole in the shutter

a ray of sunlight
studied for months

` reaching sources of emotion
beyond the limits of all subject matter'

people in the park:
a beautiful woman who tells me of Coleridge's line:
"alone, alone, all, all alone"
a woman's face known to me by photons

photons burnt onto a photographic plate
in the image of the suspected Viet-Cong
his head blown outward by a bullet

look in a mirror, try to frame that face
over your face . . .

and what are death, or photons,

                       or turns

the mind makes

            shuffling its deck of images

try to feel the photons
the photons that move thru the mind

         "beyond the limits of all subject matter"

a name for an abstraction or substance, traveling
singly and in packets

              that impinge on thought
or are thought

certainly
the granular shapes, dots, etc. . .

to know
something solid

            impedes the flow
of something not solid

and what flows between two hunks of living flesh
is not imaginary

        just not known

unless
one sends a bullet into another

                and the images collapse

for death takes in no picture

but in love

        the eyes meet *upon one double string*

                the wherefore barely known

the hint is that we come apart and come together

and are focused
in the other's heart

          and the print

              on the mind

more real
than a summer's day

and
we see
what we can

    but through it

          often
until the film

          stops

as at 4:21 PM, I stopped one film, the film of the dream
to begin another

        separate and distinct

as the people
caught or fixed on park benches

not necessarily looking at,

          or seeing each other

each frame isolate as their lives are

but a lonely gesture to the next

TELESCOPE SUITE

say I wanted you
in that room

on that cold clear night
and couldn't have you

say I looked at the stars

say there was love in the sky
but it wasn't enough

        —a young woman, a Dane,
        tells me of 5 years
        drifting in the US, of a shack-up

        under cloudless prairie skies
        looking past her lover's shoulders

        at the height of it
        her eye caught the fine stellar dust

        sparking in the upper air
        in long luminous tendrils

        and she suffered then a terrible
        kind of peace and estrangement

what she meant was:
on the star map

there were forms
in dotted lines

inked
round the clusters:

Cassiopeia
Andromeda

      or that one might see
for himself
in the far-flung galactic arms
images of women, the nebulae's vaginal whorls
or in the "black holes"
the sex of the universe itself

an old, an untrue relevance

but that one knew

they
were always out
or nowhere

vivid and trembling, but out
—though
of hurt or wound there was no escape

no need to look
nor hope to find
a sweet Elysium
of astral tides

lifting lovers to their wants
the world's sore wants

that nakedly confront

—but in star-light
star-crust
diadem

out which being looks
hidden behind Heraclitian signs

they were small
and gathered

on the silvered glass

break it, break it

into discourse and pleasure
focus and delight

or there was nothing
. . .

but that the eye, until one got used to it
was nearly closed, and no one

believed in the star on the reticule
or its existence momentarily
                          on the rods and cones

or what is somehow touched
by the mind
                  though between points
they drew straight lines
                          later to correct for curvature

because space is

and curves around

to let us pass

from one property-less void to another

so they say

and it is inhuman
that I feel such loss

and know the feeling of the vacuum . . .

huddled on the planet
huddled in need

with eyes
turned out

so that they seem gathered on the lens piece
gathered from the mirror poured from
molten glass
and cooled slowly for years

a narrative in the glass, the narrative of ourselves

never enough

and the worlds and stars drift
the computers give them meaning, meaning enough

but the vacuum
is unexplained

say I loved you

I did not wonder who we were

neither the visible nor the invisible
of what was meant . . .

on Palomar
and on Wilson

in the cold air, the shining domes

or the great dish-shaped nets hung across
the Southern valleys

I can imagine them in daylight or at midnight

open as our arms are . . .

PARAGRAPHS

1

The duck drapes its head gracefully over
its back. Then, after an instant in which
its neck forms a supremely natural arch,
slips its head silently under water,
after which a percentage of the body
follows. Ponge, who wrote of *L'Huitre*
and *un coquillage*, is pleasantly evoked
by the re-emergence of that part of
the duck formerly submerged followed by
the duck's bill in which there is a water-snail
After some time the duck which has waddled
onto the grass, or at least that part of
the duck once wet, is again dry.

2

One does not come into being in the
manner of a rock. That that manner is still
a mystery does not disfigure
the discrepancy. The rock, if it at
some other time, was not this rock,
had, at that other time, an equally
enviable condition. That is, for itself
it has no history. I imagine the repair
or heal of all that is, i.e., Creation,
to be the attainment of just such a similar
state. Thus, to be occupied solely with one's
own sense of presence which means to live
without consequence.

3

Finding sense to change. Making
form as from the last form. Being
beast after amoeba. A panoply of
shapes hints at the processional.
If things come, then go—as the
Sage relates—a sense of passage stays
the purely inevitable. Certainly the
mind in its final shape will efface
history by finding an ability to
neatly end itself.

4

Looked at from a scientific view-
point: do not imagine, do not
represent for yourself, but acquire
the qualities of a giant red star.
Cooling in intergalactic space, the
great web coalesces—its mode asym-
ptotically parallels the end of
Duration and the beginning of a
glorious Entropy in which conflict
is not eliminated but is no longer
contextual (a steady state). Space,
that other product of the Angels, will thus
continue to exist. That is, with the
universe, all you are (or all they
are) will go out. Grace, then, or the
notion of such *sans terminus*.

5

In every great rumination, one discovers
the same death. The poets grow in a
brittle age, most talkative when at
heart most silent. They know how each
word is a shift of matter, yet how
beyond them, of itself, matter
moves, and how that energy is Joyous
or Tragic but always Comic. This, then,
prepares the future corridors of the
years, a time softened for our coming:
the air, chromium at the windows, our
bodies experiencing the imprint of
stars.

ON A WALKER EVANS PHOTOGRAPH

The suggestion: what is need,
is the terror of the poor
less simple
than the man's embarrassment
as he halts in speaking
looking for a word
feeling he is nothing
until he finds it

So too, the liquid eyes
in the photograph
of the hungry face
are the center
of similar nothingness
but mark it
existing
beyond speech or promise

THE AUTUMN OF APOLLINAIRE

From the Riviera Bar
The world spreads out

On car-roofs grey-sky images are carried off
Turn corners and park for the night under streetlamps

The trees bear the cold
I'm not that cold I can drop leaves
And hibernate

For the Chinese poets this was the way
The brushstroke of ink and character

"a style of leaves growing"

Or leaves falling. The growing to old age
Hair falling in a style of leaves falling

It is a different age. No poet
Will die as beautifully as he lived

The leaves lie curled on the ground
As though their stem-ends tried
In a spasm once more for the tree limbs.

Here is 7th Avenue running North to South
The cars take the clouds downtown on their backs
The way Satyrs did beautiful women

The buildings cast their shapes
On the steel-sheathed magnificence
Of Lower New York Bay

The water is dark and gives nothing back
It flows determinedly to join the Atlantic

The salt in one's blood leaps
To join the salt of the ocean

INCONTINENCE

1

EGRESS DOOR—the stencil on the module—

opens to let two men out
who have traveled from one rock
to another

the scene scanned by a camera
to be replayed and replayed

with only minor distortions in images

that are fixed
and fixed

2

and make small mirrors
in the viewer

to which his nerves leap

the crowds at terminals
and beaches

before the massive screens

are given back
themselves

and draw comfort

the rocket's "plumed tail, that many-headed hydra"
the "lumps, chunks"
the newscasts
the words dovetailed
to the matter . . .

3

but emptiness flows in past the hatch

contaminates . . .

and when
the landing site is turned
from earth's face

the motors hum
the small lamps flicker mirroring
the forgotten lyrics of stars that winked on earth

but now in the heavens
stand steady

—in the unreal starlight
arms and limbs
curled beside the hardware
look strange

and thought itself
catches on the nothingness

—the broken open
-ness of space

that finds us
most ourselves

4

and they say: "launch"
  they say: "nearly missed it"
    : "double heart rate"
    : "looking great"

recognized and radioed
there and returned

the necessary
the unnecessary information

yet how does one
send the silence back

or the night
that breaks from a man

in whose mind
there is no metaphor

no counterpart

but the heart
grasping singularity

going out

FOR DORIS

Not ever to let it be
        I think of silverfish
skittering across a pond
        ripples
sky and trees
        but not disturbing them

as when it struck you
        it struck me
the mind mirrored world
        a way out of unhappiness
not happy
        as one might say: I'm
so happy, but a depth
        to hold
        the various possibilities
your face, mine
        there
tendered, tended.

THE PROCESS

for Michael Martone

they are in the room
she naked on the bed
and as he comes for her
certain images are loosed

yesterday, in the same room
his friend—
the camera between them-
sighting thru the optical chain
of shutter and glass

catching
or fixing him
stopping for an instant
that process

but from his insides out—some terror of openness
following his friend's hand
the friend suggesting where to look
yet, to say to himself, it is me
I wish
truly, I do wish myself

and the other man's lens
sears him to the film

in the moment when the densities,
the pressures, heats: the light
of the present

is caught as past-tense in the emulsion
this a fantasy
playing on the web of nerve ends

casting the heart to the image
one no longer is

which is a death of dream
as in ancient tales:
                              can a man
meet his ghost?
                         or can the ghost, so he must see himself
uncompleted
                    meet the man?

and fearing his ghost's death
meet obliteration?

but now he wants her
and faces her needs, saying
see the photos of what I am not
now before you

fixed in those images an acid to flame his own desire

those old stories, the ghost
hidden in the tree, took in their minds
their shape
and who left—it fell with his leaving

or they burnt the tree
and watched the gods flare loose

(what traveled out of him
and up the lens

not him, but how he knew himself
prepared by his images

and came to her, her thighs open
the sweet dissolution
that could come true

heightened and reaching
and breaking faithlessly from himself
                    into the beautiful

THE GARDEN

Sunlight at a window
Doing justice to a wall

A harsh light
Toward which low shrubs grow

Leaf over leaf
Without thought

In that light
The white cracked imperfections
Of the wall
Are its perfections

And one looks for
The minute hand or second hand
Or shutter
On which this
Might catch and fix

And the light
Makes fabric with the leaves

The objects are conveyed
As opaques and transparencies

And shiver out
Their moment in the sense

Until in time
The dark
Falls across the face

And the lover's face
Is given also to the dark

Ah, fragrance,
Thick as the throat gets
Thinking this

Sitting under trees
An orange fallen from the branch
Both bitter and sweet

Of nature
Neither happy nor sad
With how things are or are not

The past I think of
Promised both everything
And nothing

I see us as we were

Looking down at our reflections
On the garden's pool

Thralled
To be given that back

MADNESS

1

tales, dreams and signs
in things; their stories
arrive when we do

a voice
marking hearing
embeds itself in the static
of transmission

so many stories
so many peculiarities . . .

imagine a bell-shaped mouth
emitting a bell-shaped scream
some level above the noise

this real noise
telling us more
than it should
of ourselves

2

you can mine a person
as the earth is mined
from the depths up

and some assayer
call it fool's gold
or the gold that makes
fools of us

so I hear her words
everyway, anyway

and as Laing might say
it's not the `complex'
but the context

3

meet any man or woman

from the hands or eyes
the physiognomy, the topology
of gesture

by which some constant
beyond talk talk talk
is betrayed

yet how to speak of this if not to say

that in this love
the river of me beyond words
confronts the river that is you

and we are now swirled, now held
now stilled
in those eddies

4

you screamed
a terror
you hardly know of

brushing back
behind your face
sitting inside you

like another
wanting to be flesh
of your flesh

I tried to reach you
it drew you back

you slumped alone
in the chair
little one

defeated
by even those
who think
they love you

you screamed
fuck me

I was to come
into another
your eyes locked

on that childhood
of saddened animals
of monstrous-headed dolls

I felt your heart
strangely calm
beating with the weight
of two

beating for neither of us

5

what then
to be taken
at face value

the message
the sender
or receiver

and if the words
are precipitates
—in themselves
precipitous

rare and expensive dust
desperately grasped
in the amalgam

I search your face
to find the flaw
—the glint
of that divorcement
of utterance and feeling
for beyond the malleable gold
of what one hears

is the rarer hardness
of the diamond

shattered
by the misplaced tap

6

that delicacy, that frailty
of the pain of feeling
abandoned

and I too would have abandoned
my self my life . . .

yet seeing her
beyond her voice
which wove
like a deathly sonnet
entwined itself
within the webbing of myself

heaving and sobbing
the babble of terrible stories
rushing past

which lift and buffet us
—isolate particles
suspended in our fates and faiths

BIRDS AT THE ALCAZABA

1

so it might end
so it might end and all things
lose distinctness

above streets
above the brown oval of the bullring
above treetops, the wide blue
space to sea
shredded by sound

thousands of birds
screaming down the sun

among them the peacock
its almost human shriek
which, by that, still touches . . .

it is an old world
we have come to

to think
the shock of the known
the imagined as known
enough to hold us
—as the sea and metal
hold its light

we come here on the ferry,
watch the dolphin's
graceful plunge

we stand on deck
in harsh relief

blinding sun
grinding down details
of skin and pores

and the dolphin's body
thrusts down the waves
is lustrous for an instant
in the sun

the pang as it dives
self-contained
the sea wipes away its passage

in that terrible light
to barely see ourselves

the thick glinting cliffs
of strange continents
encircle and confront us

3

it was our place
it was not our place

and like those storks
which abandon their nests
—some shift in brain matter
meaning they roost elsewhere
this year, maybe next—
we come here to explore

to perch ourselves
on these rocks

above the coast
and the sea
and its beings hidden in the mist

for the eye seeks
with unclouded remembrance

seeks the world
enlarged
beyond all dimensions

the roof, the sun
under which the mind
staggers to the next thought

and the heart and lungs
scratch on the thin air
like gills
of some landed fish

an unquenchable synapse
which knows no answer

4

it was ourselves
and the end of ourselves

the house at night
its lives twisted in the bed sheets

and I walked
the parched silt hills
knowing neither you nor anyone

grateful when I knew
the path I was on

its stones and shade trees

yet the night's sexual spell
was cast across the days

we went out
we returned
we may have suffered

and surely we came back
as different people
but to a precise feeling
which sustains us

5

the almond and the oleander
on the roads at dusk

the paths which spiral
towards fortress walls

yet we come here
and find
the transplanted Sequoia

the transplanted swirls
of Arabic art

we come here to partake
of the transplant
of beauty . . .

and the birds cry
their tremendous noise
—polyphony, do-decaphony

—thought tries to place the sound
yet nothing in the mind
can contain it

foreigners in a foreign land

—can one call another foreign
who in that dusk
is tremblingly clasped

for the otherness is beautiful
and terror and delight
in the same moment flood the heart

KNOWLEDGE

(1979)

I

VISITOR AT ACABONAC

Last night's rain
Washed mud into the estuaries;
Today the water is burnished, impermeable,

Non-reflective under the sun's flat hit.
Down the beach, some distance from the bathers,
Gulls walk along a sandy ledge.

The moon afloat in daylight,
A chalky hallucinatory eye
Above the tide's grey dead sluggish weight,

Suggesting only
What is isolate, what cannot link. This is
A world of forms, of manners

Of voices and cries of birds
Shredded in the reeds,
In the stunted pines:

These intact islands
Amid these minor eddies of the human
With their small distances to be spanned.

At the harbor mouth,
One comes upon shingled houses
Desolate on hummocks, on low spits of sand,

And the white sails of pleasure boats
Catch sun like perfect messages,
Perfect dreams that ply between.

THE TOAST

Dapples this glass, the wine—
The hearth coals
Embered flies in its fine crystal

You across the room—elbow
Or strand of hair, pinioned
In the reflection
Amid red liquid, amid red glowings:
Difficult loveliness—unknowable star
Of this warm composition

Let the eye go
From there to you? Let it
Break from the glass
Where lingering spares the shock
Of the next mote of deadly beauty

And now, there's but a word,
Another pledge of the voice
Which bears despair in its tremolo
As we both swear to the image unproved
Meant to shatter
This refracted prison

KNOWLEDGE

To think a man might dream against this
This something simpler than metaphor

The world
Which spoke back
In facts, to him

That heavy pageantry

Yet when the life or when the bed
Was empty
He'd lay his head
Among the voices of the dead

It was his child and his childhood
It was coats and books
Heaped in a room
Toys and an ache

LEAVING GRAND CENTRAL

for George Oppen

On the way to a sunlight of lawns
And suburbs, to find oneself caught
In the train's swaying,

The smudged window's thistling
Of a few lights. At the windows,
With faces set.

To look out past
Dusty reflections, past
Girders crossed and blackened with smoke

Which hold the roof, the careless
Heaven of the paving above one's head. This
Is not our world, one wants to say,

This channel which will spew us
Into a daylight of blocks and blocks
Of utter ravishment.

And as the bridge is crossed
In the windless day
Barely a current moves

Under the imaged buildings.
And what little guilty cry the heart makes
For safety in escape—

To be borne past
The towers and low rows of flats,
To see behind the brick and glass

Those trapped in the real apparition—
Here the window does not mirror back.

FLORIDA LETTER

They come here
To repeal a northern drabness

To find frivolity
A recompense of straw hats
Of colorful clothes

They want the sunlight
Which dispels the chill

But the hard glare withers
The eye slits on death

Watching the wave's glitter
As it eats away the shore

Only time itself is the obdurate
Against which the heart leaps

And the white hotels
Are like bone against the sky

This was no one's future
No one's dream

Only the poor power
To make a dream imaginable

QUESTION OR ANSWER
BEFORE THRENODY

for my father

I .

Already, the hibiscus blossoms

Its odor on the late August air
Mingling with late season parchness of grass and palm

By the canal's edge
The reds and browns
Are given back their mirrored figures
In the almost still deep green

Already, the lizard skirts
From bush to bush

Its eye in its round horn
Alert to light and shade

And do you see the blank sky's whiteness
Mirroring nothingness

Or the pale blench from color
At the red hibiscus's center

I I .

Small triumphs surround you
The photos on the wall
The plaques and gavel

The darkened brass
Inscribed with names

Trophies which halt nothing

Your goodwill
And virtue are not mine
To judge. Rather, I see

Your face pinched,
Tears at your eyes
Perhaps you foresee
What cannot last:

This youth, *this* strength
To gaze upon
Your sons and daughter

These shred-ends

Disentangling bonds
Of the human

I I I .

Story of our lives
Like the story of our differences

Like beach glass
The sea throws up among the shells

The filmy winks of purpose

Father upon father—
The chance-haunted voices—

Together for a time
We live out this resort life
Of beaches

Together
We found it foreign to us both

Even today, looking
At the wall of palms

The road's turn
And the bay holding
A more vivid moon than I remember

Who can say
This world?

I know of youth
Spent and respent

And the eye follows
The efflorescent track

To the sky's white stone
The stars melt in its light

Never has it shone so much as now

For neither love nor indifference

Miami—NYC
Aug.–Sept., 1975

II

BIALYSTOK STANZAS

from a book of old pictures

1

Light—
The scene filled with photographer's light

This sparsely furnished room
In the corner of which
A china-closet Ark

The old men
Under green shaded bulbs
Reading Torah

The prayers are simple,
To what they think larger
Than themselves
—the place almost bare,
Utterly plain

The flat white light
Adds no increment
But attention

2

He sits in the armchair
Beside his bed

In his hands
A Yiddish paper

On his head
A high black
Pointed *yarmulke*

The room's things
Furnished by donation
Reads a small brass plaque
Above the headboard of the bed

A bed, a hat upon his head

A *yiskor* glass, the candle for the dead
Burnt down, the wax scraped out

He uses it for drinking

3

Shiny linoleum
You can almost
Smell the pine oil

The beds
A few feet apart

So the old men
Tired of the world
In the evening
Can face each other
And talk

But now the shades are half pulled up
Sun streams in the windows

The room almost empty
But for the two directors
Sitting stiffly on chairs
Who, like the white painted beds,
Seem supremely
Official

At one side
Two grey bedridden men
Finished too with dignity
Are giggling

4

The old bind with phylacteries
—between the leather turns
The pinched flesh bulges, the old
Skin, the hairs burn

As if to do this is also
For the pain
—to explain
To Him of what it is
They are made

Thus, why they fail

5

This one and that one
Look like madmen
With their long wisps of hair

They scream: I chant, I dance
Like a crab

In the room the women wail
A plangent erotic note
Their loins itch with double fire
As he in topcoat-who-is-blessed
Bestirs them
Screams their demons back

Until their innocence
Stands naked as desire

Oy, Oy
He whirls, he spins
Till the beard is out
From his face like a flag

And in wild wisdom
Throws her to the boards

She, who would
That next instant
Have pulled him down to her
But for the trick
Of the ritual

6

THE JEWISH FIRE COMPANY

There was one fireman none knew
Neither his family nor friends
He had good eyes, though they looked
A little wild. He was sent
To the watchtower

One day, almost at once,
Two fires broke out in town
The Hasid grocer's
And a gentile butcher

The fireman warned
Of the butcher's blaze
But said nothing about the grocer
Whose place burned to the ground

When what he had failed to do
Was discovered and explanation demanded
He said: those who do not
Follow our God's way
Must be helped
And those who do
Must accept his justice

— — — — — — — — — — — — — —

This one joined
So the young ladies
Should see him in uniform

They did
And flattered the brass and the leather
But not him

Finally, he charmed a farm girl
Of pious family into the fields
And in the manner of the orthodox
Threw his cap to the hay
Where he thought to take her

To his delight, she bent toward
The straw, raising her skirt
As she kneeled. Suddenly,
She whisked the cap up
Tucked it in her girdle and ran away

So ashamed was he
The next day he left for Warsaw

Years later, the farm girl
Placed the cap on her first-born's head

TERRIBLE PICTURES

Page 147

Snow—
A group of people
Awkwardly caught

They have just discovered
The photographer, and he, them

The old man with the sack
Who has turned
Shrugs his disbelief into the lens

No sense of emergency
In the pose
Could be as real

Grimly
They lie closely packed
Upon each other
In the mass grave

Looking now
Like figures of saints
Carved across cathedral doors

—but beyond image or irony,
The empty wrongness.

Here, all death
Was made untimely

Page 163, Caption:

"fought in the streets to the very end
and perished by his own hand
with the last remaining bullet"

Page 164, Caption:

"died in the ghetto"

Page 166, Caption:

"fell in battle . . . 1944"

Page 168, Caption:

"killed . . ."

Page 157, Burnt Synagogue

This light—
A river through which
Another life poured

Figure and ground
Of how the dark
Informs the light

Brings forth bodies, faces
Brings forth
The things of the earth
That we see to completion
—beloved, hated—

But that life was broken forever
Here, look, look, this is but
Its mirror

Only the mirror remains

And gone—
Whole peoples are gone
To horror beyond remonstrance—

Freitogdige
Donershtogdige
Shabbosdige
Consumed in those fires

Words can add nothing
That flame itself was without a light

The Yiddish names above were those given by the citizens of Bialystok to the victims of three mass executions: "the Friday dead," "the Thursday dead," "the Saturday dead."

8

FROM THE ZOHAR

The blue light
  having devoured
All beneath it:
  the priests,
The Levites, etc. . . .
   Now the prayerful ones
Gather
  at the flame's base
Singing and meditating
   while above the lamp glows,
The lights, in unity, are merged
Illumined world
   in which above and below
Are blessed

9 (C O D A)

S E N I L E   J E W

One God. One boiled egg.
Thirty *dy-yanus,* and the Paradise
Not yet given a number.

Eight nights, eight lights
Which break the dark
Like a cat's wink.

I think the boot is not gone—
Whose boot? I ask
Do you wear the boot?
Or does he who wears the boot
Wear you?

Coat of my pain, cloth
Of pain, winding sheet of
My horror. Just a rag,
Just a *shmata.* You
Are not my pain, not you.
My pain is me: I am the Jew.

III

AFTER MONTALE

Nothing which seems particularly large.
The poet catches the mere termite
Busy at its burrowing. Then that fellow
Disappears, and only the hole
Is left.

All this took was time.
And we wonder what it is
That time itself creates or excretes
Or simply disappears into. What hole
It leaves.

DRESSED STONE

In the image sought
As something so primitive
Something it must have said
To those who looked
And from that articulation
Things had to be named
And the mystery held in love
By that name . . .

So, in winter
The slabs lie jumbled in the snow
Half-exposed beside the building site
Their aspect fierce,
Close to the monolith
They've been cut from

Until employed in the design
And thin tar strips
Placed between saw-marked surfaces
Where as night falls
A slight shift of temperature
Will take a meaning

Then the eye, by habit, strays
To the moon
Riding the unsheathed girders

And how beside use, how
Close love must be
To the cold light
Touching stone
Across the distance

THE MIND'S RETURN

to D.

Do you remember
By this small river, the Seine,
We had come

The sun was setting

In the light which held
The building stones glowed red
The heat was on the air
The air one breath respiring

This true, unalterable . . .

In that place
Our bodies partook
Of that dreamlike dance
—the strict simple principles
Of density and mass—
Substance of the mind

In that city, where histories and their dying
Are equally grand, equally absurd
Those engendered phantoms
Pressed from the heart
To inform the real—all we will know?

How we bore those marks
The living and the living rubble

Yet nothing at last seems ours
Different, that is, from being mine or yours alone

And the mind seeks
Among those signs
Rising to the rigor of the world

Where the glass of buildings flared
In the sun's fire—
A sheet of flame—

And the stone
Was for a moment after the sun set
Still warm to the touch

MÁLAGA: THE PALACE GARDEN

I think we have lost
The theme which is recovery

But the source
Is followed out

The trace of branched duct
To flowerbed and pool

To seek the thing
Which forced this shape
Which feeds so much
And determines so much

To find it inconsequential
—some pebble
At the gate of a sluice

There, the water whirls
And discord lashes in the channel,
In the beveled stone

And what is lovely plays against,
Against even the discord
And the discord imparts to it
The hidden harmony
Thought better

Yet this is still
Not the wonder
Which annuls
The iron ring in the wall
Or the shine on the Guardia's leather

And here the stone rests on stone
And we want to note that this thing matters:
How the builder's art has made this place

So the sea wind blows back
And mixes salt with the tree's fragrance
Along the flagged walk which runs the rim
Above the city

Down there, the bull dies, I suppose,
That the bull-god may live on

Yet we have found it hard
To picture dungeons pitched in stone,

To imagine for the unbeliever
The gilded Allahs of that page
Were heavier than the sun . . .

The music of the caged birds,
Of the water's purl
Is both sad and joyful

As is the burnished handiwork
Of the chambers of the King
Before whose doors, power withers love

Above is the frieze, the running lattice
Of the grille,

The trapped energy of image

Fearful nuance—by this
Are we lulled from terrors and greeds—

These acts
Which would supplant their beginnings
With their consequence—

Yet in time one is trapped
Between the beauty and the fault

Evil is victorious
The wheel does not stop

The quarry's stone
Shows even in the chisel work
The unmeant markings

POEM OF AMERICA WRITTEN ON THE FIVE HUNDREDTH ANNIVERSARY OF MICHELANGELO'S BIRTH

Freedom, after all? The train
Moving through *the land of the free*

From the embankment: the highway,
The tract, the house: destiny's

Manifest. The senator on the podium's
from sea to shining sea, which now

From any small vantage, such sense
Of sadness. A few trees

In the straight ruled streets, barely
The hint of contour, as though

The world were at last possessed.
Movement and stasis. The buildings

And shapes under the open air.
And the dust from the railbed

Glints in passage, like the slave's
Form, half-carved, escaping from the rock,

Edges aglow in the museum light. Finished.
Finished. Dust

Dancing in the air in the knowledge
Of limit's time and limit's place

Tormenting dance of emergence.

AND IF THE TRUTH WERE

and if the truth were
that Icarus sought
the sun

wouldn't it also be true
that his father
passed on that love
to the boy
as fathers will
—dooming them both

so that Icarus died
perhaps as the old man
would have wanted to

while Daedalus went on
like a youth
with the bitter mockery
of invention

IN THE PARK

On the bench,
Sitting in the woman's lap, a grown man

A *pietà* seen
At ten removes of time and place

Making the story's end
Suddenly its beginning

Mother, I remember
That red peaked broken union
Which was your breast

And know no older wound
Of memory

Invited and lost,
Invited and fled

And my life again a broken tale
—not for truth, but *to please you*—
Which I have to tell

AT ALBERT'S LANDING

(with my son)

I .

The path winds. You are around a bend
Unseen. But your voice
Crackles in the walkie-talkie
You made me bring. "Here's a leaf,
A tree." The detail,
Not the design, excites you.
I don't know what to say.
After months in the city,
I'm feeling strange in the woods.

I I .

Spongy ground.
Matted leaves
Beneath which lie
Dirt, bones, shells.
Late April: milky light
And warmth. Thinnest odors rise.
In the middle of one's life
More things connect
With dying, what's come,
What's over.

I I I .

It is said
That what exists is like the sky
Through which clouds pass. I suspect
That mine is a poetry of clouds.
Above me, some wispy tuft catches sun
In an interesting way. *The naked very thing.*
I'm glad of this, don't look
In the billowy mass
For the teased-out shape
Of a horse's head or a bird's wing.
Yet finding it now and then,
Unsummoned: some thought or image,
Recalling how each
Depends on each.

I V .

Together we follow the trail's twists
Until the pond.
There, two white egrets
Stand against the high brown grass.
Intent watching
Is almost timeless, but some noise
One of us makes scares them off.
They rise over our heads, circle
Out of sight. Strange sadness
Grips me. The after-image
Of their shapes still burns.

V .

Here we are in some fugal world.
Tree branches make a kind of tent.
And the squirrel, when he eats,
Looks like a little man. And here
You fling your arms out
Whirling around at the frightened
Skimming ducks. The duck's eye,
Like ours, must be its center. We
Are alone, rooted in our aloneness.
And yet things lean and lean,
Explaining each other and not themselves.
I call you; it's time to go.

V I .

Different as the woods are
This is no paradise to enter or to leave.
Just the real, and a wild nesting
Of hope in the real
Which does not know of hope.
Things lean and lean, and sometimes
Words find common centers in us
Resonating and filling speech.
Let me know a little of you.

I V

OBJURGATIONS

1

Talk in the room
The voices thick with lyric

And to hear the facts bend in
Deflected from the absolutes
Of wall and floor
Of limit and definition

To speak of things
In terror
In the brutal cognates
Of love and desire

Until, like the floor's worn boards
Beneath which gape the hollows of the building
One's meaning gains some small shine

2

Rooms scar the mind. Empty rooms
Which punish for love. Yet the place
Is fulfilled, indicative . . .

Shut the door, draw the blinds—
No closure here
But that of carpentry

The walls, the bric-a-brac are heralds
And extend themselves

It could as well happen beyond these walls
As well in the world, the part-willed
Of the world . . .

There, to have arrived severally
Perhaps interested
To consider exchange

To equilibrate the goods and lives

To watch the crowds move, reflect
Make over their movement into purpose

To walk, to be buried,
To be huddled in their bulk

To go from them cheated and hated
And to hear later, others felt that way . . .

Yet, in the numberless storms of event
To find no one
Who meant that this should happen

To watch them moving
And the moving
Either lovely or ugly

To discover cause
And no place closed to it

To read from the street signs, placards,
Shops, the days of traffic and trafficking
Seemingly impossible of error

Thus, to fear a mystery less than certainty
To fear the terror of explanation

To impose rules, to judge,
To discover motive and reason
To go beyond reason

Until, like the monkey in the photo
One is stranded on *The Structure of the World*
Grinning from that bare pole

4

Which is
The danger of the literal

Meaning:
To search for what you might love
—not what might love you—

To find up close
It is still what it is

To know the gods have fled
To know myth only as this moment

To know the breast
Which bears your head and your humility
Is not your mother's breast

This is the danger
Of the literal

5

Where is that moment
When the poem like a worm
Painfully parts the tissue

Spiraling down the psyche
Dark turn on turn
Toward some light of true cause

Finding, nibbling, feeding on that cause
Till it's we who are the worm
In the poem, and cringe in its light

For this is how the world
We call beautiful
Came into being

And the worlds through which
We move, even its trees and rocks
Are the absurd works of men

Things to which
They have given beauty
Only half theirs to give

And it is conquered
Even with ecology, finished
And only that not begun
Not by us at least, has any power

6

Thus, whether the word is found
Or finds us, it is inserted in history
Though now we are told
Is no time for a *bon mot*

To suspect and not from error
That one seeks an identity
Of a mathematical sort

Standing in the world,
Functioning as some imperfect
Equal sign

Because both sides of these equations
Always balance—there is
No other way to look at it

Therefore, the horror must be let in
And like Tu Fu, one keeps
Music and rites to conquer his failings

To keep a machine clean
In a filthy time, to seek
Meaning for compassion,
Meaning: don't let self-definition
Perish

To be condemned thus
From the beginning—no time
When it was different and not different

No time when
All this seemed more expendable

7

Like the newly hatched duck,
Placed beside the basketball
—took it for its mother—

That we're determined or not
Is beside the point

If we're born
With attraction towards a thing
Even the wrong thing
It's also towards ourselves

Neither the mob at the spectacle
Nor Homer at the wars
Is a singular

If I must prove this
And not do so by exception
—that I, for the sake of hatred

Might have lusted for a woman
Then grew to love her deeply
For having let me come

Isn't it to say, the poem
Is now and then our master
It bears our beatitude for what's most unholy
Even our outsized hate

So *thralldom!*
And the whole schema
You little shits

Which I would bomb and bulldoze
If I were King

Ha!

8

The cities and the bluntly shining stars
Clusters that can gleam with use

A dispensary: *grab for them*
The thing we're taught

As indeed, the last word
Of the poet's reading was "stars"

And after, we walked to the pier
One star in the sky

I said it was Venus, imagined
It the star

Which gathers love and world

And in the half-truth of the metaphor
The point it holds is clear and steady

And yet the small lights in streets
The strung necklace of the bridge

No more than complement

9

Light among buildings
Catching the sharp edge of stone

Familiar yet isolate:
He, this brick, this city

Stories in the streets
Places given names

Memory and fantasy made real . . .

To feel one had the meaning wrong
The error not of increment but of tone
—not of the Gods, not even of their house

But we had seen the thing like a god
Or like some manufactured part
Sitting in the sun

Yet to tell of the difference
Between our worship of the dream
And the worship done in dreams

To wake in that room, that world,
The sky grown light

The spectacle of building tops and streets
Plunged in monstrous otherness

To know meaning and remembrance
Dwell no place
But in the blood

V

POSTULATES

Loss is more complex than gain
Though neither completely understood.
One remembers
He was five, six, seven years old.
To the fact of the memory
The memory stands
As an axe to wood. Wood, ourselves,
In the streamings and contours,
The roughened grain.

Make a mark on me.

SPECULUM MORTIS

Angled toward you in the glass,
Mind wanting ease
I think, Mother, we scarcely look alike.

And yet, the `doctor of grief'
May do no more than be a little slothful.

And the light is
As from a non-reflective dark

And invades the mirror's space.
A hollow strangely lit,

A light, sourceless,
Radiant

As any truth,
Disfiguring all one thinks one is.

STELE

for Jane

Otherwise goes past all object
The light blazes on the stone

The light which also falls
On you
         And I touch you
Almost as I touch death
Following where the light goes
My voice half-raised in respite

And I know then
What is beyond an earthly love,
What escapes the chisel's work:
The hurting godhead within the stone
—all that we wish
Might want us—sealed away

And when thought and sight
Are taken to the marble's grain
—held there by cupidity of beauty

That death I know
Is but a light on form

INTERMINGLINGS

to J.A.

I .

Sun on the begrimed windows,
Light and dust curiously arrayed.

Infused with each other, falling
On the bed, on ourselves where we lie.

Finite life in the pattern's
Verge and shift, in the hovering dust.

In the beam's slant,
Designs almost infinite.

I know, in my heart,
This nature is all aesthetic.
Each, resolved, being something like a story.

Story of ourselves
In these curves and tangles,

In the half-light.
What I wanted to say

Was that in truth, we each
Could have picked, could have
Found ourselves

Among any of these.

I I .

Many years given
In belief of the body's sadness

A thickness, as of the throat,
In the world.

From there, the voice telling
Into its knotted web
Of glints and darknesses.

Perhaps you are moved as I am,
Lifted in some strange way
By the plunge into sorrows.

Facing each other, these recognitions:
Two small animals, quiverers,

Aware they can be hurt.
And sometimes, nothing,

Not even the severe lines
Of your body, which wildly delight

Bring me this close to you.
For all that is different,

How each in our life
Is alike.

III.

We agreed. No one's quite written out
A philosophy of affluence, least of all
This affluence I'm feeling today.

What strikes in the world.
A curious kind of comfort

Where bug and leaf, or better, bug
And garbage in the street, are joined.

The broken hydrant almost sings a warble.
The undersides of clouds, sulphurous green and red.

Crossing the Bowery to your place,
"marks of weakness, marks of woe".

Strange, ugliness and loveliness
Both slash the heart.

No shelter: we are exposed
Like the weed shooting through the rubble,

Like the tree's small roots
Which curl at the stone, at the broken pipe work.

Almost part of, and not against.

To imagine this
Is what is workable.

That the spring did not come
To enrage the tree . . .

And I think now of the open bow of your back,
Tremor which ends, which does not end.

The gesture sears.
The cursive graves its line in me.

This remains the one gift.
This alone is unconfused.

I V .

All this living, dying.
The town lights seem barely pinched
Out of the folds of darkness

And the moon, so lovely, so far,
Full-blown tonight into a dream's indifference
Riding solitary above the black pines

The skunk waddles and the deer
Comes to lick at the salt block
Ghastly in the whiteness, perversely
Monumental—

They move with the rest
Through the eye's frame of
This beautiful pointlessness

I too arrive without exactly having
Taken myself—my *self*, whatever,
In this moment, that is.

Where, that depth?

And the chart and the star book
Are strange counsel. The fixities themselves
Are caught in their slow turn
And go under the world
Like human time, like human death

The candle sputters, dies in the room
Burning all, chair, bed, bodies into shadow
—breast, thigh, you, me
And the light and dark pour their grainy liquid
Into that wave that bears up love, succor, pity
In a transmigratory arc

ON THE BEACH

I .

My doctor tells me:
With your skin, sunlight is dangerous.

Western Man, I'm hurt, but go armed.
A broad brimmed hat, umbrella,
Lotions which I am told stop light
But draw flies.

Sitting there, I read that Montale saw,
A la Fellini, a monstrous woman
Plump herself down onto a crumbling sand
And speak Truth.

I try to spot truth from shade,
Watching square yards of such flesh
Baste itself with oil.

Thou shalt be anointed
For glamour, youth illusion,
The thing to do.

What I see is that the sun is bright
And that perhaps suntans, while looking
Healthy, are deceiving.

Even here, amid these minor increments
Of peril, one is consoled. In this
Careless resort life of beaches
Deceptions themselves are a kind of truth.

I I .

The philosopher tells us
Mentally we are joined to what we look at,
That seeing can haunt.

If the wave is rough
One sits it out, bathing
In the shade or sun.
It's as free as this other thing
The mottled clacking teeth of empty shells
Can hint at.

By the path's edge,
The infectious tick
Sits on the tip end of the dune grass

Like one's gaze,
Ready to be fed
Ready to install other infusions.

Above, seabirds wheel—
Not so much cruelness, but what is actual
In eye and beak.

Overhearing that line of Rilke's
"You must change your life."
I looked again at the sea's glint.

III.

Depending on the weather,
Yesterday's sandbar
Is today's dangerous shoal.

Yesterday's clam,
Today's 700 beats of a gull's wing.

The high rump of shingle
Where the sun fell, in the instant
When it fell for everyone,
Is also gone,
Dredged this winter to make
A boatman's channel.

It's not all mechanics, all improvement
Or all evolution.

Depending on the weather,
We play a funny game
On the beach.

My son follows me, stamping his feet
Deliberately into my tracks.

He says, I don't want to step on a sharp shell
                                        or jellyfish.
Laughs, Look, Dad, I'm crushing your footprints.

V I

STANZAS ON MOUNT ELBERT

Where we climbed in the berserk air
Of trails, sharp spiky views
And dizzying vertigo. I watched
Marmot and pika dart
Among lichen-covered rocks
Envying not their agility
But that they survive
On such apparent bleakness.

Then, seeing you on the path above,
Aspen crook in hand, orange poncho
Bannered to the wind, the painter's
Famous *Wanderer in the Clouds,*
Whatever passes between us,
Whoever you are, in that moment
You were a guide to me. We took
The path six inches at a time: with each
Breath a step; with each step a breath,
Sounds of ourselves reverberating
In hollows, in great brown cratered cups of rock
Until what was human seemed to be passing
Into its sheer facticity.

And by the summit, head abuzz in thin air,
Pain or joy or confusion heaped as one
Into the round bulge
Of the mountain's endlessness, it was
Almost too comical to have walked there,
To worship at that feast of obstacles.

And the lakes four thousand feet below
Leered crazily. I think
We were looking back
At what does or does not exist,
What the mind mirrors; something
To which we do not so much return
As turn to, though the turning hurts.

FIGURES OF SPEAKING

1 .

From Norman Malcolm's memoir:
"Wittgenstein like to draw an analogy
between philosophical thinking and swimming:
just as one's body has a natural tendency
towards the surface and one has to make
and *exertion* to get to the bottom—so it is
with thinking."

Sadness, love, intent. These too are heavy.
The poet also not a fish
But an aquanaut in a dangerous medium.

2 .

In a book on the ancient world
Reading how grave robbers don't dig
But drive a bronze rod
Into the ground
Until something they hit
Makes the right sound.

I think
I rob my own grave
When I look at you
Writing a word, Losing myself.

The marvel in the unexpectedness,
Not so much sound as recognition—
As when I found you in a mural
In that same book,
A wraith
Who 4000 years ago
Danced beside the Indus.

3 .

The beauty of the older poet's voice
Punishes me.
What is beautiful must
Or one doesn't believe it.

4 .

The *whoosh-whoosh* of the inhalator in the hospital room
Counseling patience.

5 .

Hearing her sing to herself
I knew it was not an aria of the sexual,
Notes of which we would both mount . . .

Rather, it was the quiet hum
Of the quotidian
Self-involved

By that, saying
I am me, who are you?

6 .

My little boy.

When I hear him trying out
Words he's learned

Impatient to reach
The matter,

I'm reminded of my own going in . . .

Not all words sing.

Thinking of poems,
It comes home to me
—the world already existing
Without a name.

MOURNING BY THE SEA

"sough incessant"

Your father died, mine dies.
Mothers, sisters, brothers still.
Dark harbor water mottled green and blue.

Before us on the sand,
The crab claw severed,
The bivalve crushed, the shell in shards.

The *on* then *off* of this is hard.
The place,
The boundary edge—

Where picked from off its ledge
The polyp dissolves
At the gull's stomach wall.

This is not spring; this is not fall.
The brush tips all.
Your eyes, your laugh—

To see one living is to see by half.
The body changes before the eyes:
Dust dark in light the sun burns.

Such light on waves is curve and turn,
End seeding end.
And the image then that wants to come,

Thin as air,
Is nothing but words: terror and fear,
No self and no recurrence.

NEAR GUERNSEY

In the guide book:
The account of a Mormon woman

Trading her wedding ring
For a sack of flour

To know
What's not in the story

How life exhausts
Each symbol, each ideology,
Leaving only itself

Not that something thought sacred
Was traded for bread

But that the bread thereby
Becomes the sacrament

SEEING THE PAIN AGAIN

`Personal' histories.
Like seeing black bushes
Against the night

Or the moon's ghostly
Paring of itself
Swirling in clouds

Almost the reversal
Of identities, roles . . .

Nothing to turn from,
Not even the pain I can't answer for

Here in the mountains,
In the clear air,
One faces the whole thing—
Yours, mine—

An ocean's worth,
Suspended
Amid the great waves of rigid stone.
Something in which the whole can barely move:
Shocks, faults, tides of shale . . .

Thinking of how each is hurt,
Even if it is past, even
If it is no longer seen or touched,

Contact remains.
It ravages in the confusion between us
Like a storm at a distance

Undecipherable, private
But for the lightning's flash
Which lets one see nothing but itself

Releasing into something true:
One dark outlined against a dark.

MANHATTAN SPLEEN

The trees: knobbed fingers grasping at the grayish mottled sky. We had come from downtown to see a friend who was appearing in a ballet, and, since there was time before the performance, we, like others around us, sat on the benches before the massively constructed concert halls, pale stone edifices which seemed designed to defend the arts rather than house them.

As we sprawled there taking some pleasure from the fresh air and an occasional piercing dart of sun, a dark-suited man with a terribly deformed face came walking by. It was an unusual deformity, for though the skin was clean and unbroken, one could see that the right side of the face was involved in some gruesome disease which had swollen the jaw out of all proportion. The illness had perhaps destroyed the eye above the jaw, for the man wore dark glasses and under the right lens one could see an eye patch, really more like a cup than a patch. The man's jaw worked constantly, quite apart it seemed from any volition of his own, as though it were ruminating on its own condition. But he went by, and as he did, I thought how in this city, the grotesque, both physical and mental, is frequently encountered.

Actually, it set my mind thinking of certain artists who often exploit physical disfiguration to indicate a kind of moral corruption. I was thinking in particular of a rather well-known film director who loved to make use of dwarves, of maimed and scale-eyed beggars in all sorts of tableaux. Such things can be effective in a soft and sentimental way. An audience, gripped by horror, will make an easy equation of physical and spiritual corruption, a fact which politicians and moralists have not ignored (indeed, one thinks of all those examples of the wages of sin inevitably depicted in terms of venereal disease or insanity).

Now wounds, it strikes me, may properly bear such a function, and yet how rare that is! For one may gaze somewhat ashamedly at the ambulatory veteran or the armless sleeve of a uniform at a parade and the spectre of social corruption will truly fly into one's brain—along with the image of bravery, etc.

But then, even these thoughts momentarily slipped from my mind as we entered the auditorium to see our friend dance. And sitting there in the darkness, I felt that very palpable thing, that pervasive eroticism of the taut beauty of the dancers in motion. Imagine my sudden shock then, after enjoying, after being absorbed in that severe grace, to have the house lights come on for the intermission and see, sitting only a few rows away, the man with the deformity, sopping away at his lips with a handkerchief, his jaw working furiously like a pestle in mortar.

Curiously, I looked at the people on either side of him wondering how they responded to his presence. For where else but in great cities— now huge mill-ends and heaps of chaotic regularity—does the grotesque strike with such force, if we let it. In cities, where arrogantly we think (or thought) ourselves masters, the grotesque plays its hand with all the arbitrariness we though conquered. Nevertheless, the people near the man were ignoring him.

See the contrast I suffered here: the impression of those superb bodies in the rigor of an art form, as against:

> the man's wish for a finely chiseled jaw
> of lips which could be controlled long enough
> to bestow a kiss, dreams of impossibility
> that link to the thousands of dreams
> of being other than one was

How we were joined under the weight of this accidental insufficiency no more explicable than health and wholeness—that jaw ever-working, a *perpetuum mobile* of pain itself!

In that moment, all I could feel was contagion, a desire to leave.

But then my friend, who is often of amazingly good spirits, as though secretly reading my thoughts, pointed to the man and said, that must be the Critic. And he laughed and I laughed, but weakly, and only for my friend's humor. And when the performance ended, I hurried my wife and my friend out of the theater, making sure we took the aisle farthest from where the man had been sitting. And outside the air was fresh, *was fresh*, but the clouds tumbling across the immense panes of the building glass threw me again into a panic.

IN THE BUILDED PLACE

(1989)

*Circles and right lines limit and close
all bodies, and the mortall right-lined
circle (Θ The Character of Death) must
conclude and "shut up all."*
—Sir Thomas Browne, *Urn Burial*

I

WITH A TELESCOPE IN THE
SANGRE DE CRISTOS

There
Where the mountains bulked
Above the valley floor

And town and ranch lights
Made shallow bowls
Into other heavens

Raw nature actually seemed less raw.

Again and again that night
The glass checked
In its round frame

The nebula's thumbprint swirls:
This fine life of bonds and connections . . .

Then
I looked in
At another's eyes

Looked past that image
Of the self,
In at the pupil's black hole

Where light gives up
The granular,
Becomes a maelstrom

Grinding
Beyond the phenomenal
To a lightless, frightening depth.

O this fine life of bonds and connections . . .

FATHER PARMENIDES

Neither great nor small
The hollow simple is.

Like the wine of its cask, the voice
Empties the speaker, empties
Even the void at fullness.

MOON STUDY

To steal a look at it as the tide pulls,
And the earth, sheathed in the living
And non-living, bulges and dimples

At the surface of the seas. The moon!
It appears beyond my capacity
To do more than give it name, to shout

Like the haiku master, O bright!
O bright! O moon! as though
With a word I could embrace

some lucent teaching of its being. To have
No hold on this architect of shadows, this
Realm of space, of airless peaks, fantastical . . .

America, tranquil and monumental under
the hard moon, is also a dream of cold light
Raining purity of cities alabaster.

And now, sister of the obdurate,
How the body of love gleams otherworldly,
Exotic with distance and intimacy. O pallid!

O nightmares of wars and terrors, O terrible
Bright! The great pocked surfaces,
Craters of the moon, craters of the bomb,

These two texts have swallowed *cri de coeur*,
Ode and epistle, our books of loss.
In the restless night, at the window,
My white ego meets that white eye.

CORAL STANZAS

after Mandelstam

O city, o white filigree just below the grainy depths.
Can it be a reef which absorbs the star and moonlight?
O reef, am I flung, cast toward shoal, toward beach?
Is there water clear enough, soothes enough
Surrounding the far-flung branchings?

Bitumen pellicates fester in the vision,
Falling like hell-snow, falling like hell-snow.
O into depths, more depths, your brother animal
Swims into poisoned channels.

Brother animal. o white filigree, city of Venus.
Light mote and tear duct festering in the hell-snow,
In the scurried depths.

THE BRIGHT LIGHT AT THE POINT

to G.O.

Read the words of the African tribe
on the civilizing of the world:
"this earth has lines upon its face,
scoured marks upon its ground"

and walk in this
eye-piercing light,

the sky a guillotine of blue,
world severed into edges:
water, shore, two houses on their separate dunes.

And I am cleaved, lined, marked off
against the century and its full
blown dreams, its fantasy of control
as though the world were caught
within the body,
and every thought or hope swam
locked within the oily mass.

Cicatrice sadness here,
where, way off, bells and buoys
cast their lonely moans into the world,

for the light—this modern light—is piteous,
sheering and estranging clarity

lest each one shipwreck on one's self.

AT BEACHES AGAIN

1 .

To have heard:
Indians made escape routes
Through this dense cover of gnarled pines,
Paths snaking under matted poison ivy
To emerge in sunlight brilliant enough to cleanse.

To arrive at this beach
Where Marconi set up his wireless
Among the dunes. Foregrounded

Before the sea, three blistered iron struts
Bolted to a concrete base, rust flakes
And stripped nuts scarred by the wrench.

The long bleached stretch of sand
Is not unlike Kitty Hawk further south
Where the Wrights launched and the Indians there

Had long since

2 .

Lovely, these spots
Where waves come in, go out,
And the clouds are banked at the horizon

Like another mass of coast.
The sky then adrift,
And one can imagine messages,

Signals, as we now signal stars,
Coalescing out of salt washed air:
An unseen human tincture

Of news reports of them
'dying over there.'
We, in our own way, of course, are dying,

But there are many ways to die,
To come back, to survive
Our incontinent desires and wars, many ways

To re-enter certain deeps, though
We taint even the run-off of continents
And make of this ocean

Something more than witness,
Make of it a communicant.

3 .

Imagine, as he said, "the light
holding for an instant . . . "
Enough to make one get in the car,

Drive out to that bluff above
The bay's sweep, to find
The view so magnificent, truly

No one need be standing in it.
And the little world of the head
Is brained like a drum

Against this light swept other,
Is suddenly error
Fallen out of time,

Vague solipsism
to the counterpoint
of the foam-tipped sway of waves.

And the beach edge bakes in sun, the space
Suggesting endless stupefying lethargy.
There, a coiled rope, a drawn up boat,

Signs human but also of the sea.

4 ·

Times when the jukebox true?
That fractious music!
When the sentiment is free

And the heart goes for nothing
Toward some extravagance of words,
Times which obsess us and our disappointments

Are terrible. We have come to the time
Of the accurate missile, of concern for such
Accuracy in the world, of all that we call terror.

Even love is poised on that pelvic
Terror, on the wave and its sparkling foam
One barely hears in the world.

We have yet to hear that wave break,
Hoping we are shoreward enough
But that we are overheard.

For speech, speech comes with ease to us,
Yet what if there is more of that wave in man
Than speech.

5 .

In the classics, man was added to nature
To make an art both bitter and sweet,
An art not good for us who stand here.

This cliff edge leads outward
Towards the deepest blues of space,
Worlds of history at one's back—

The dead and wasted centuries.
And here one can manipulate the gaze
So that the gazer finds himself expendable.

Hölderlin spoke of these high
Marine lookouts where no one wants to be.
And Lorca, as a child,

Would walk into the sea
Only with his back to the waves.

The last sense here
Is the sense of taking leave.

6 .

Woods into which the Indians fled,
Dark as a closed book or the death-flecks
That cling to the mind's sheer open

Brilliance. And the wet black kelp strung
Along the sand is already maidenhair,
Dragging the eye down, vectoring
Towards the waves, away from the light.

And the beach is wide, wide to the water
And swept by winds. Possibly a bird
Marks fresh tracks over the dune's ripple,

The spiky shadow of the weed
Scythes even this brightness

THE ACOUSTICS OF EMPTINESS

What the ceiling absorbs.
Possibly that which I don't want to hear.
Noise over hollow, over self-abyss, chatter
That clucks I'm a chicken before the axe falls.
Anxious, I believe it. The nerves are a lush playing field,
A gaggle of neurons, well tended in the pilot,
Swathed in the formal blankets of discourse in the diplomat.
Yet what I hear is the mind-forged mumblings of tyrants:
"flowers," "democracy," "he's human"—that's chatter!
The paneling with its punched holes holding the hearsay,
The old clichés of the poem, like worshipping silence.

IN THE BUILDED PLACE

"I wandered thro' each charter'd street" —Blake

In the unfair life
Of this night or any other,
In this city,

Someone's broken world,
In the streetlamp's
Small circle of light,

To find no magic aura, no blaze
Of clarity on the broken littered pavement,
To find neither justice

Nor penance of lives, to find
Only the absurd arrangements and disarrangements:
A slum block in the light's cool bath of truth.

*

Who will it hurt that tonight
This broken world is but a literal?
Who will it hurt to note

The light on a woman's face?
To see her face pend in time?
Can it hurt to note

The weight of time
Weighing down the lovely features,
Unable to break loose

From that which it weighs upon.
It suggests no more than you resolve this:
The gross weight of life in time

Looking to be resolved in meaning,
Solved in love.

*

Tonight the clatter of failed myths,
Of hierarchies, dies. Tonight
We are joined as one in the street lamp's light,

A corrosive light: dissolve, dissolve,
Discovering selves in the core of world,
That lonely need. So that we may arrive at last

In late dusk, in late time,
Bare islands of the human archipelago . . .
I stand back, watch the light on the curves

Of her face, not so much to feel
That rush of movement in me,
As to see again the quick and the alive

Open under open air.

*

And the sky's curve
Lies against the curve of the city.
Streets, people caught in thickness

Of event. And the eye and mind are led
To the moon's loft, to the bird aquiver,
To the serpent's gentle coil.

That they connect,
Connect like consciousness
In concentric whorls

Or like stations of the cross
Through loves, hates, errors . . .
These flimsy beatitudes of order.

ASTHMA

When the slight rasp in his throat starts up
My nuclear war-time goes interior, fills the whole head.
The shock-waved halfway house of hope de-domesticates to splinters.

The stores on the mall are so much bought hambone of desire,
Rorschach's of the mental wobblies, the local sales centers of sex,
Ingestion, *dégustation*, flattening in the in-rush of punched air,

Uplifting the fear bird's white wings, the smothering clutch
Of feathers that cram gullets. And the young boy
Whose sweet life is a keep, is my bank overdraft, my

Joy vault, he, who is not yet even historical, and so
Expends himself in file-throated shout, in play over
The junk-food city, the toy torture of the TV

That makes an idea as political as sliced pie
Or Psyche's credit-card sorting of seeds, laying
Down diet, health, avarice to store coin for

The dim video game of winter. And the child's
Cough, not the madman's speech, is so irrational, so contrary,
That black squander of air, that thick squalor

Where in this century most air is stolen.

WELL-DRESSING ROUNDS *

—Ashford in the Water, Derbyshire

Terrorists leave notes
on dead bodies, warnings to others
not to touch, and I remember that Antigone,
against Creon's published male tyranny,
sought to set her brother's body at rights
not with other men but with the earth.
Possibly, the city man, out in England's
green fields, puts his hand to the grass
as though touching a pliant woman,
as though renewing a pact.

Here, in Ashford, flowers blaze,
bedeck the fields and woods.
And again, my hand sweeps as though
to gather this world to the fable book
where it once lived. But I'm a tourist,
with my own stories, walking
to the well heads and to the bridge.

Last week, a printed handout reads,
school children gathered plants
and flowers among the trees,
pulled petals from blossoms,
plucked seeds from pod and husk,
gathered tufts of fur from rabbit pelts.
The teachers must have shown them how. I read,
and I'm with tourists, whose nations
divide up seas and lands while we walk
to well heads and to the bridge.

Hands of children shaped
the crude, broad Marys and the Christs
with outstretched arms made of flower
upon part of flower, corn and pea
lining borders, all pressed
into now dried plaster. They ready
this bloodied world as though it were
a benison, *rise up o earth*—
the message as we talk and walk
round the basins of the wells.

Flowers are everywhere in Ashford.
It is midsummer; children dance the maypole
for visitors who come to walk the circuit
of the wells. Water rises up; it sparkles
in the sun, water of which we're made,
of which we drink, and this is what they honor
as we walk from the well-heads to the bridge.

*   *In certain towns in Derbyshire, the ancient wells are dressed (decorated) each year during the period of the mid-summer solstice.*

AFTER CLASS

Swirl, swirl, the leaves which Shelley summoned.
Desiccate the dead leaves across the park. Mr. Wolfgang,
Mr. Wolfgang has stopped me after class and dances, on
Toes, a dead leaf dance. And the bare trees are armature
Through which night descends. Who is in the park
But student, bum, tourist, visitor plastered like leaves
Against the dark. Mr. Wolfgang: "For fifty years I lived
In Berlin," and swirl begins. I look at Mr. Wolfgang's face,
But there is nothing that I ask. "I read," he says,
"that American's poem about a jar of glass. My head
Became that jar, so last year I came to *Co-net-e-cut!*
And now I'm here." Infectious swirl, infect swirl,
ja ja that jar. "Professor Heller, I must tell you
Something funny. I studied law for years. One of my
Professors made notes from another's book, then wrote
A book of his own. He did not know he wrote
The other professor's book. He was arrested."
Swirl, swirl. "It's so easy to get infected." Swirl.

I hear the dead leaves scrape my voice: history.

II

MYTHOS OF LOGOS

First the stars or the patterning of stars in darkness, and then perhaps someone climbing up a mountain to close the gap. Begins in dusty foothills, then forest, then high empty tundra and piles of rock, and at the top to brush at with the hand the spangled emptiness. But the hand feels nothing, sweeps nothing but the cold air. The loveliness of blackness for the first time brings solitude. And then one keeps silence at failure, nurses anger and shame, swallows the bitter taste.

And so the world becomes another place, and now I must confess to the many things that I forgot to say, was afraid to say, for fear, for love, for shame, O ancients and splendid hosts whose words come before and after,

Who have uttered out, one theory goes, what was written in the gene codes and in the stars' imprints before our speech. And now, those lucid structures are gantries to my nights, wheeling and reassembling.

And yes the whole career is night, is crafted out of silence. And so the sentences out there were not unsaid, nor did they blow away with stellar dust and stellar time. They settled down about my head, resembling a dome the exact shape of my skull hidden from others by a flap of skin.

AFTER PLATO

To the poet: not to be original.
No heart can fully voice itself.
No public so bemused to follow.

How to bear a poem whose truth
Would sear the sky, a bright sun
Rising per schedule. More heat,

More sweat, more guilt to add
To toil? Poet, spend your days
Surmising cloud banks of which

There are a vast sufficiency.
Praise occluded forms:
Your blinded loves, your hates.

Too dull? Too milky in their lucence?
Think of horrors when in the calm
Someone thought they saw the light.

Squint and wait for shifts of wind
To put shapes on chance maneuvers.
Ah, ruins afloat! See, your little

Nostalgia requires no contrastive blaze.
With luck, clouds will break
To rend familiars. This, the more-
Than-moment of the blinded reader.

As though, for you, a god
Had meant us sightless. As though
An eyelid had been peeled back
Only to insert a cinder.

HOMER TIMELESS

His way was not his way, but being blind
His way was that much more attuned to death.

Some called him camp-follower; others claimed
He justified Achilles' gloom, the tide of which
Had thrown down cities.

At the pyre, Achilles had Troy's twelve high-born
Slain. "This," the poet said, "was an evil thing."

Yet he also showed the bright blade's
Flashing beauty. He was accused:

He did not report the real war. The listener
Listens, remembers what he will remember.

*

It is said the wave-break off Hellas metronomes
His lines. What more noble than this mime of giving,

More honorable than to stay with his words
While outside, beyond the chair, is flesh and rubble.

Take the gift of his rhythms.

And after one is emptied by war, knots
Of one's stomach nodules of ice, to imagine

Oneself among the maimed and rotting, the beach
Where once the sea was red with burning ships.

They could not go home. And while he spoke,
The Greece he spoke of made new Iliums

As new found lands make new births.

RILKE'S SONG AT THE WINDOW

"Why am I weighed under this infinity?"

Depth-charged
Blossoming sea

Wanting force to surface
To bundle what's locked in:
Tensors, magnitudes, stripped nuclei
             and burst them forth

And how clear one can draw lines:
To know I could not help you
And you bawling your head off

Into those shadows which were your past
And I searched myself to retrieve you
And I'd vomit up myself

And now I know the dead in life
—the dead we have brought with us—
And the stifled death of words are one

Terror is molecular:
That otherness we fought for
Was but this
virulence of ourselves

PHOTOGRAPH OF A MAN HOLDING HIS PENIS

for Michael Martone

World o world of the photograph, granular,
Quantumed for composition in the film's grain,
But here blurred, soft-toned and diffuse
Until the whole resolves into an ache, a
Chimerical, alchemical flower, a pattern
Against pure randomness.

As though the process itself exists to mock
What is discrete, is singular. Dot leans on dot,
On the binary of *only two* can make of one a life.

And the myth is partial,
A dream half of need confused with desire.

I too live out this fear, this shadowed aloneness,
The white hand's delicate hold where the genital hairs
Are curled, the groin become a hermitage, a ghastly
Down of our featherings . . .

And the texture is bitter, bifurcate,
A braille of flesh
From which a ghost is sown.

TODAY, SOMEWHAT AFTER DANTE

The wind is blowing; the wind bends everything
but the human will. Thus war and pillage
have written more on the earth's surface than wind.

The Wars, Vietnam, the Greater and Lesser Holocausts,
these names, like those of the Florentine treacheries,
season whatever paradisiacal truth to poems.

Yet, today, I fall like a blunt object into respites,
walk forgetful among the wind-blown shrubs
and brackish estuaries on this day of unplanned sun,

happy to be lost in the world's things,
in all this matter and *dura mater*, to feel
when I speak, in each word, a sweet tensile pull of a string.

Afternoon light is penetrant, a blank, absented
fixity. What birds have flown off I will find
in glossaries; old loves I will find in

the mind's book between a cloud and a branch or
a filament of moon in the intense blue. And perhaps
I will stumble, as in a vision, on all the dead,

mother and father included, lining the shore
of Little Tick Island where they will be busy bowing
to that figure of perfect freedom, their self-same minds.

And in the distance, like a memory
of love's midpoint, I'll see the sun flash white
on the salt-caked weather sides of twisted trees.

HETEROGLOSSIA ON FIFTY-THIRD

Streets of a city, I walk and lose the hour.
Today, unsure of what I write, I circumambulate
the new and the ruin, find it
twelve noon amidst museums and gleaming limousines.
A bag lady shouts "I am entitled!" I also
am entitled to my thoughts at least, yet all day,
dream or nightmare do my talk, undo my walk,
so I let talk pitch self into doze or dream and chat:
man, woman, testicle, dessert. The language falls,
a chunk of disembodied sound through space.

My body sometimes feels like a corpse, but talk hears talk,
and I 'm entitled in the streets, astride the century's
fatted calf, the pavement-glutted bowel. The talk of
street people is a groaning, each to each; I have heard
them singing on the trash. Ghost words, ghost fuckers!
They utter their words right out to do their ravaging
in me, joining my dead lords of speech like animals
granted province over those on whom they prey.

IN CENTRAL PARK

See, the bee emerges.
The furred dart sails
Across the grass, its whirr

Lost in the greater buzzing.
Like us, an after-trope
Is visible: hives, structures, cities.

Is the gatherer of nectar
A bourgeois or a communard?
Am I supposed to mind which?

Today, I read of one philosopher's
Impassioned hope. "Domestication,"
He writes, "is irreversible."

Above the trees, the high-risers
Float, perforce, before the sun.
In the streets, the comings and goings,
The endless traffic . . .

What dance there is
Must be saved for within
That honeyed fortress.

JURY DUTY IN MANHATTAN

That the law is blind, lovely and precise,
but that the blade rips air below the balance.

That the room reeks of municipal staleness, and so
thermostats are checked. That father-right and property

are base notes to legal melody. *Oh yeah, oh yeah*
is hummed by the young man called today.

And that the sound of killing time entombs the room:
the lawyer's drone like an artist's shoptalk

about the end of composition, the mural's tugboat
frozen midstream in paint between Liberty and the city.

ADULATION

for A.S.

"Adulation? Why, it's the structure of the world," said my friend. "Something more complex than mere appreciation."

As he spoke, he was studying the expression on my face, for there is nothing he enjoys more than to make a toy of my understanding.

"Listen," he went on, gearing up to provoke. "You've trained in the sciences. Imagine a statistical study of applause as it is heard these days at concerts or performances. Imagine measuring that pandemonium which contains everything from climactic relief to the feel of one's ticket money well spent. I may be wrong, but I notice a nearly obscene animation on the part of audiences no matter whether the event is any good or not. Dance, music, theater? Those sitting in the seats produce, as though under contract, oceanic tides of claps, howls, bravos! And the objects of such applause are required to stand, to bow, to bring themselves before the curtains, to front the mobs while severed from their performances and roles like butterflies forced back to being caterpillars and chrysalises. What truncations!"

"But," I returned, "you make it sound almost like some game, some ritual of formalized gestures: show ends, audience cheers, that sort of thing without regard for content."

My friend snarled: "A game? *Oh no!* In a game, two play, two get hot from the activity like two sticks rubbed on each other. There are sparks, fire, interchange! In today's auditorium we have a different system at work: one-way energy, parasitic leeching, pig-hunger, zip going to zap but no zap coming back. *In today's auditorium,*" he began to raise his voice but mastered himself, "the audience's psychic recesses are muddied up as by a stick, swirled in a swamp. It's out and out piggery: 'oh dig into me, into my wild striated unimagined livings, etc and etc . . .,' the audience croons." He paused, then went on. "Adulation is *ex post facto* foreplay."

"What are you getting at?" I interjected.

My friend played at being lost in himself. "Those flushed faces," he sighed. "You know," he suddenly fixed on me, "I have had the fortune, good or bad, to be invited to numerous benefits, the kind where in the name of some worthy cause, rather well-off but otherwise undistinguished people gather in some public room with a sprinkling of celebrities, a famous conductor or playwright, for example. What occult occasions. At one side of a well-carpeted room are a gathering of *nouveau riche* anonymities, and there, across the velvety spaces, perhaps with the organizer of the function, is the renowned guest. These two sit on armchairs in semi-repose affecting intimacy while little by little the adulators leave their small knots of friends, these drab pigeons, and drag their long faces like broken wings or like glowing piglets to nuzzle at the guest. What abjectness must accompany this activity; no one can come away clean from such an encounter, even while it reverberates with its mystical dissonance. 'O dazzling reflector of my soul,' that long face mutters, 'o exemplar who breaks the mold and makes more human my ownership of seven supermarkets in Scarsdale.' The celebrity here, you see, is a kind of wondrous mirror, giving back the life before it *precisely* by containing all that is behind the mirror, all that would utterly flatten the pigeon standing before him. And so much the better if the pigeon, through some quirk of commercial awareness, should find in the haughty features of the famous, the flaws, the vast ennui or the facial tic by which the prince of the people may be brought down. Surely what is operant here is the fantastic love of one's own clay which turns every utterance of praise or understanding into a verbal backstroke!"

Now my friend, with this tirade, had made me a bit uneasy. I had only the other day been standing before the portals of Grand Central Station watching the well-dressed commuters piling through to catch their trains for the northern suburbs. I had thought then of the immense skies over suburbs, of their soft light, of autumn over their houses, that light in which trees seemed to dissolve and stars appear as free miracles, of the crisp dry leaves on the ground. How delineated were the sky, the brick, the stone walls of houses with lamps at the windows, shelter, nest, the furrow of a known woman. What a miraculous thing it must be to return there after the theater with a vanquished feeling in one's chest. Adulation! Adulation! It seemed the nearest thing to death, I wanted to cry out, thinking of the sonorities, the textures of having touched the hem of greatness. The immaculate cleansing.

My face must have displayed my strange feelings.

"You know," my friend said, "it doesn't end there. No sooner have these people returned home from their gala, then the phones begin to buzz, 'today I was at a cocktail party with you know whom . . .,' 'how wonderful, let me know when such a thing happens again.'"

My friend had a great smile on his face. "Then the networking begins! Soon an entire world of pig messages, of this piglet love-talk is going on." He began to prance around the room, oinking and snorting, with dramatic sow-like turns. At first, I imagined he was doing this for my benefit, but no, he was losing himself in his little game.

Beautiful, beautiful, I thought and began clapping.

Whereupon he stopped, turned, glared at me and left the room.

Nevertheless I was sure he would call me the next day.

STROPHES FROM THE WRITINGS OF WALTER BENJAMIN

In shutting out experience,
the eye perceives an experience
of a complementary nature,

less the product of facts
firmly anchored in memory

more a convergence in memory
of accumulated facts,

the replacement of older narrations
by information of sensation.

According to theory,
fright's significance
in the absence
of ready anxiety.

FOR PAUL BLACKBURN

Living between the boulders
Of the world

That grind down
The boulder of the self

There falls the fine powder
That comes of grinding
So soft it is to touch

False softness

Roll this rock back
From the damp ground
Through which water seeps
—the rock become
As frangible
As earth—

And the worm bores entrance
Before its time

MONTAIGNE

This bundle of so many disparate pieces
is being composed in this manner:
I set my hand to it only
when pressed by too unnerving an idleness,
and nowhere but at home.

I want to represent the course
of my humours; I want people
to see each part at its birth.

I have grown seven or eight years
older since I began, not
without some new acquisition.

Through the liberality of the years
I have become acquainted
with the kidney stone.

It was, precisely, of all the accidents
of old age, the one I feared most.
For my soul takes no other alarm

but that which comes
from the senses
and the body. I have at least

this profit from the stone:
that it will complete what I have
still not been able to accomplish,

to reconcile and familiarize myself
completely with death.

The more my illness oppresses me
the less will death be something
to fear.

God grant that in the end, if its sharpness
comes to surpass my powers, it may not
throw me back to the other extreme, no less
a vice, of loving and desiring death. . . .

I have always considered that precept
formalistic which so rigorously and precisely
orders us to maintain a good countenance
in the endurance of pain.

What matter if we twist our arms,
provided we do not twist our thoughts.
Philosophy trains us for ourselves,
not for others, for being, not seeming.

It is cruelty to require of us
so composed a bearing. Let this care
be left to the actors and teachers of rhetoric.

If there is relief in complaining,
let it be so. If we feel pain evaporates
somewhat for crying out,

or that our torment is distracted,
let us shout right away. If we play
a good game, it is a small matter
that we make a bad face.

IN THE SCHOOL

Open window has a grille.

Air going by assails.

Sky's blue, piercing through,
is gloom. Teacher's defensive tone,
textbook poems he admires: celebrations
of the West, Frostian walks in woods.
"I write a few myself," he tells me
"when emotions hit . . . my father's death,
the day my nine-year old said 'don't
touch or kiss me . . .," pauses, looks
towards shelf. Light falls
on close-packed spines of books.

Screams and shouts behind us
in halls and yards
        and voices raised
to an inevitable almost sexual hate
because the air which fills the room
is not the window's air
which in its passage seems like the words of an art,
roiling desire with its touch.
Our lives are out of reach.

What air remains
is high in the children's throats.

SESTINA: OFF-SEASON

These are the poets' times, these dark times,
for the world takes as real its own fanatic thought.
A realibus ad realiora, the words build a hexagram
of stagnant heavens while peasants do their work and fall,
the superior ones do their managing and seek reclusion
in their summerings beside the sun-blasted light of the sea.

The poet would rather borrow from the moon-puddled sea,
but how give up the coiled worm gnawing at the times,
burn up the page, put the word in reclusion
until only the sandy coasts are objects of a thought
and history can be thrown for a ten count fall
—the cry of nothing—of ghost birds, cage, a hexagram

for poets who hexagram
their luxuries beside the sea,
who swoon and fall,
whose visions are multiples of love times
lovers, endless self-circles of thought
in secret fondness of their reclusion.

O poet, car roofs and glass glint under leafy reclusion
and one must give heart to vocabularies of the hexagram.
One must be at pains to see the world glitter in mere thought,
to see the cruelty in the lives of animals and in the high seas
of our leaders' rhetoric which downs the very times
and makes of these last grace notes a mechanic fall.

Compose; if necessary, compose against the fall.
For god's sake, leave this elysian reclusion!
Note how sea-scud and bird-lime mark the times,
how the lines flatten to this one sad hexagram
of hope, the moon's pearl puckering a violent sea
as poetry despairs of any cogent thought.

That poet who warned of unsightly sifting sands of thought
entered into the very end of time's articulated fall
where every word is borne upon a flood as if heaven's sea
were an earth of inundated lands. Uncover! Mind performs reclusion
as though recounted lives were pent beneath a hexagram
of yarrow stalks, spelling, in emboldened crumblings, our times.

Too long is the word disembodied from our pain while reclusion
buffers body. Unbuild this great vast hexagram
whose rigid lines misprision poets from loves' times.

III

OUTSIDE A CLASSROOM IN NERJA

"Ayer, cinco pescadores morir"

Grey clouds massed
over waves and horizons.
Light bands itself to peaks
and to the sea, an enormous
tarnished plate their boats must plow.
Existence, a constant birth of signs
rising toward this, their outward life,
febrile, thinner than air, idea
no more than a glimmer unless a word
slams home its bolt.

In the narrow streets,
walls painted with flaking lime,
where at night, children sit
in front of firepots and see,
in the maze of lines, clowns
or dancing bears—faces carried
to bed with delicious frights.
The ever-readable randomness.

In the morning, to stand beside
the school, peer through the window glass.
No inklings of the lessons. Only
to watch the teacher talk, the teacher
who has the eyes of her poor dumb
fisherman father, eyes which look
at the children as he looked daily at the sea,
the same small anticipations and terrors.
        Perhaps her words catch the waves'
dead glint, but explain indifference
or recalcitrance to a child?

And now the small gyrations
of her hands, as she tells something
to the children—whatever is being
said—are as beautiful
as the wind-shaped clouds
above the mountains.

TOURIST'S CAVE

1 .

Stood on the floor of stone
The names given to the many chambers:
Hall of the Cataclysm
Hall of the Cascade
Hall of the Phantoms

Stood on the floor
And the lights, the lamps of red, green, yellow
On the stone flutings and the water-worn

And the man who rediscovered the cave,
When the boys brought him to the entrance
—it had gone unnoticed all those years—
He flashed his beam down the pit's mouth
"and the light fell," he said,
"so that nothing stopped it.
It went on and on to hell itself," he said.

But hell was not there,
Was above in the air
Where one walks.

2 .

Like the odor of wild thyme
Found on the hillside clinging to the hands,
The sense of this place clings to the eye.

Air so clear
It sings the white of painted houses.

Beneath the eaves of the *Alcalde's* house,
Abandoned nests of the African stork.
Like the tourist, an erratic synapse
Brings them flocking to the town
Every four or five years going north.

And the rich and the poor alike live locked in a profusion
Of flowers; no spring, no season, but the geranium,
The bougainvillea are always there, and the not-so-rich
And the newly rich tend also
The plastic flower.

Tourist's eye of seamless pastoral.

But at night, firepots wink before hovels, lights,
Lights of houses on the hill.

"O look into the eyes,
O begin with the eyes,
                        eyes wide
In the dark."

3 .

At Larios's estate,
An iron gate is mortared to a wall
At the end of the village's poorest street.
Through bars, a garden is disclosed
Where one of every flower grows, and footpaths
Lined with polished planter's wood
Steal all the flyblown eyes.

Please—or not so politely—the villagers
Are forcibly removed.
Pitiless sun is given to this un-mask:
Not scarcity
But greed in a plenitude of light.

Removal from sunlight
Is the history of their kind.

4 .

Firepots wink before the hovels,
Lights of houses on the hill.

Where they are gathered, they talk
About the fearful night.

For it is night in the world now,
And the dark does nothing

But remind them of their own dark.

5 .

One night we came down from the mountain village by the route which followed the dry river bed, a vast expanse of white boulders, pale and dusty in the moonlight. We had come this way before only in daylight, and were now being guided along by one of the townspeople returning home. As we came to that part of the riverbed nearly a quarter-mile wide, I could see lights flickering high on the walls of the cliffs which marked the old banks of the river. What are those lights, I asked? *Animales*, replied our guide. *Animales*? *Gitanos*, he spat out. For here lived the gypsies whom I had seen in town, dirty, ragged, the children bitten by fleas and covered with sores. It was widely believed the gypsies had the power to hex or curse, and many of the disturbances such as bad weather, bad fishing or ruined harvests were blamed on them. None of the gypsies lived in town. No one would have had them, even if they could afford the rents. I had wondered where they lived, and now I knew, the caves, really great open holes in the cliff face. After dark, as one walked this riverbed, it was their candles and lanterns which one saw. And now, as we passed closer, led by our guide, we could see these lights casting curious shadows on the walls, outlining the massive rims of rock which sheltered them, so that it looked to us as if they were living inside an enormous human skull.

6 .

This to say of the neural chains
On which thoughts ride.
They too are completely in the dark,
Like creatures of a cave,
Blinder than moles that tunnel.

7 ·

"Living nights," we called them.
That whistle in high woods above the riverbed
Which followed us for miles.
One could hear it above the stream's trickle,
Above the sounds of our breath bouncing back
From the narrowing gorge's walls, hear it
Until the rocks seemed about to seize us,
The two cliffs face to face
The way no one could be with any of them
And not draw up his own terror
Cold and quick as the torrent of water
Swirling about our feet
Which we tried to shout above
For some nameless quality of contact.

.

8 .

The chambers named
The colored bulbs which play

To hell had the light gone
And in the strata, the clay pot and the bone,
The great white bone exposed in the strata

And the lamps red, green and yellow,
And for the first time, heard there,
With the others, drowning voice and time,
The piped-in music

And the drawings of the ram and of the bull
Were for years undiscovered
—such pains to do their work in secret

And the named chambers which led to "hell itself"
—the floors of which,
The bones and the axe in the strata

And the eyeless fish
Can know nothing of the light
Know nothing
Of the red, the green nor of the yellow

STATUE: JARDIN DU LUXEMBOURG

The grass tips rise, pale white field daisies
grow in clumps, green surrounded by sandy gravel,
paths, benches, statuary, students having their lunch
in the bright sun, oo la la all this in French.

The grass reads out the Father's epoch, obscure
and bound in creation's knot, and the epoch of the Son
squats in the greensward, in curved bronze
captured in upthrust: *Les Étudients de la Résistance.*
No comfort in the patina's uncanny cold, in the hollow
structure of the Patriarch's leg to which the youthful figures cling.

Our epoch is to live with these two,
Father and Son in time, to repeat endlessly
these cycles of grass and bronze. Yet Paris encircles
like our Mother, incrustations of plaster on plaster,
centuries of wear, humans stuccoed to the pile,
these little affections to outweigh a dream of monuments. . . .

The city stretches off into sun-watered light.
To be in love with this minute is to be
in love with air displaced by metal.

ON A LINE FROM BAUDELAIRE

at Père Lachaise

"The dead, the poor dead, have their bad hours"
If there are the dead, have they lived in vain?
Things continue, it all says, the stars bulge and quiver,
The neutrino beats, the oxidizing of metals
Heats modernity. In Paris, over the poor dead,
The tombstones fascinate, the cats hide in
Marble and shrubbery, the walls are like a vise
And enclose. Once they asked for flowers, too late,
For flowers. Green spring honors the living but who
Begged? The spring resonates with her silk; even gravel
Sings, the worm has turned me to poetry. The dead,
The powdered rich: names are taken. History spirals
Into the center of this conch shell, the air swirls
Over Paris, out of reach, lives on, dies on.
The airs of the universe beat oceanic
On these well set up stones.

CLIMB TO AN ANCIENT CHATEAU IN FRANCE

at Lastours

Stones spilled out of ruins
arouse an ardor in me. So hard
to climb there I confuse

standing on the precipice with
some out-of-the-century height, some
out-of-the-body jest by which to take

in the eye's sweep and laugh, at our feet
all bloody Europe. Effects of clear air
only faintly tinged with rank perfume of shrubs,

of nibbling goats. We pick our way, animal-like,
among rocks, not for bittersweet verdure but to believe
for a moment the escape from time's laminate,

the hawk made cognate with the boom
and the contrail. And then,
that brilliant zephyr of fear, to lose
the ground rock, the affection for

the elemental. And yet, with another to share,
to be here, hand in hand, thus, what to ask?
In asperous loveliness, catch breath, lie

as one in high grass, our bodies rapt
in what is present, mind vacant
as the calendar's unused blank.

The saxifrage clings, and the pattern is broken.
And possibly a word can survive like this:
a stone parted from its mortar, the discourse
of contours, striations and lichen.

FIFTY-THREE RUE NOTRE-DAME DE NAZARETH

> *"Paris*
> *Paris*
> *Of your beautiful phrases"*

I .

Isn't this the window?
And isn't this the *troisème etage*?
Just another dream above that zero base,
The hardened sites of syntax,
From which the populace's many tongues
Rise into their pain,
No two minds, nor worlds, alike.

Apartment borrowed, I have also borrowed
This language, another's plangent, torn *bon mot*,
This world, *l'écriture*, a borrowing,
And I've looked below, cut from the cloud burst
Mottled sky to see the borrowed ones of France,
These North Africans who gamble in the street.

I've been absorbed in examinations:
There, the very top of an ear,
The sculpted ebony's shiny flue.
Also, I've watched the games they play
On crate tops chalked with numbered squares,
Playgrounds of this *la malbolgia lumière*.

I have seen this from above,
For I am of the imperious gaze, the leaseholder
Of the view, and cannot help but note
These gaming wooly heads,

Cannot help but hear their click speech,
Their lover-words, their shouts, and all these
Bespeak my vantage, my political,
My pâté-laden table. Oh I have looked,

And I have seen! Disembodied tropes
Of the century's textual warpings.

I I .

As another legatee of Mallarmé,

I have strained against the tongue
Until the word displaced
The world's foreign body,

Have played with the exclusionary pun,
And yet, and yet,

Have sat and let my life go
Into this beautiful table laid with foods:
Cheeses, wines, *légumes en vinaigrette*,
Let eye catch the tin patina-ed roofs,
The balcony's potted plant, saw across
The way through gauze, a woman
In her underclothes ironing a blouse
Beneath a blazing chandelier,
In broad daylight.

And I have wondered if
The poem need witness something,
Or simply come to take its place
Beside these lovely things.

O how generous to rest
Without predator's intent
Among one's other possessions.

III.

At night, dressed in white, in at least three
Rented rooms that I can see,

Arab shop workers face east and are supine.
In white and supine, in the murderous arcs
Of nearly flattened bodies,

They face east and are supine,
jihad scrawled on wall against . . .

And this mecca is a rock,
Its hammer: a bone
Lodged in flesh.

IV.

During the day, they listen to
The cardboard carton's amplifying sounds.
One man is decorous, another's smile is sweet,
An urban gazelle's or desert creature's grace
As he shakes the dice-man's hand,
And the pleasantries are not French
Nor ritual, nor colonial *juju bees*,

Rather, cosmos is invoked
In the *brinng, brinng, brinng,*
Dice rattling in the cup.

V .

Brinnng, brinng

So much purposeful noise
One has no part in:
Machines which hum in shops
Or the foreman's edgy drone
That make for a ghetto slum of sounds

Against which the rattled dice
Sound a kind of *no one means this*;
They lie there being nothing but themselves. ·

While at best one writes
The lightning's thunderclap:
Not the event itself, but the event's
Near after. Poet, this is the husk

Already burnt, the belated desiring
Of an image on command,
O not one's own, never one's own.

VI.   COLLAGE:

"impossible not to be gripped by the spectacle of this sickly population
which swallows the dust of factories, breathes in particles of cotton and lets
its tissues be permeated by white lead, mercury and all the poisons needed
for the production of masterpieces . . . of this languishing and pining
population to *whom the earth owes its wonders*."

"Again I lean on the rough granite of the embankment
As if I had returned from travels through the underworlds"

We have come by myriad gates:
The arch at the top of Saint-Martin,
Portals, canals, boulevards,
Borders to be traversed,
Lines of poplars shimmering in summer heat.

Look down rows of statuary and buildings,
The famous tower drawing down the sky,
A brilliant landscape of gods, beasts, men
Who wander in that seamless envelope of mind.

And there are grimy courts, alleyways,
Masoned *cul de sacs*, lightless baffles,
Shut-outs.

From travels, returning to the underworlds,
To find every word another brick in these brick walls.

VII.

Chase a number until it's marked
A counterpoint of *naught*

Chase a number and fall supine.
All set things come down in the null
Against which history has built
Its concrete, its blood-stained showings

The dice reverberate with a call
To a cosmos set apart, gamblers
Conjoined to the noise-making myth:

universe, chaste and free,
made of these called up sounds
the hazard inverts the real
no longer telling hope but truth

IV

SOME ANTHROPOLOGY

And yet poems remind me of the tribe of the gentle Tasaday
who some regard merely as members of another tribe taught
to fool anthropologists with false primitiveness and *naïveté*,
to be blunt in their manners and infernally innocent.
No one is sure, as with poems, whether they are real or a hoax,
whether the dictator, in his munificence, created a forest preserve
to shelter them as he might set aside an apartment for a poet in the palace.
Forests and palaces, such utopias are mostly exclusionary, like hotels
for the rich, and needn't concern us. It is rainy for a rain forest
to house our myths, to shelter our lost tribes, who, one by one, gather
in a clearing. I sometimes think about my lost tribe of Jews, American
Jews, also part hoax and part invention, whose preserve is sheltered
under brick where limousines hum and one hears the faint, familiar
babble of the homeless. As it happens, the Tasaday are being
declared "non-existent" by government scientists so their hardwood
forests can be transformed into chests of drawers. Strange, then,
the anthropology of the poet who must build his poems out of the myths
he intends to falsify, who says, look my friend, you are laying away
your laundered shirts in a rain forest.

THE AMERICAN JEWISH CLOCK

When did Solomon (for Zalman) Heller, my grand-
father, come here, his time folded into America
like honey layered in Middle-European pastry?

When did he arrive? After his pogroms and wars,
And before my father's. Was he naive? To arrive
like an autocrat, to enter like a king, in the train

of minor victories. Zalman, here called Solomon!
With a new syllable to lengthen his name. In the vast
benumbed space of us, a little more sound to place him.

Were there sour Jewish chives on his tongue,
Yiddish chimes in the bell of his breathe?
He knew very little English, but he cocked his ear.

He heard the clock sounds that translate every-
where. He had been brought into redeeming time,
each stroke the echo of his unappearing God.

With tick came the happy interregnum,
those Twenties and Thirties when profit
turned to loss, and loss to profit.

Tock came later when the synagogues swelled
with increase and were tethered like calves
on suburban lawns. And then . . . O and then,

the young walked out, walked back
to the cities, prodigals of emptied memory.
I was among them. And the door slammed shut.

And the space outside, that endlessness to America,
was ululated on every word but tick and tock.

IN A DARK TIME, ON HIS GRANDFATHER

Zalman Heller, writer and teacher, d. 1956

There's little sense of your life
Left now. In Cracow and Bialystok, no carcass
To rise, to become a golem. In the ground

The matted hair of the dead is a mockery
Of the living root. Everyone who faces
Jerusalem is turned back, turned back.

It was not a question of happiness
Nor that the Laws failed, only
That the holy or sad remains within.

This which cleft you in the possibility
Of seeing Him, an old man
Like yourself.

Your last years, wandering
Bewildered in the streets, fouling
Your pants, a name tag in your coat

By which they led you back,
Kept leading you back. My father
Never spoke of your death,

The seed of his death, as his death
To come became the seed, etc . . . Grandfather,
What to say to you who cannot hear?

The just man and the righteous way
Wither in the ground. No issue,
No issue answers back this earth.

FOR UNCLE NAT

I'm walking down 20th Street with a friend
When a man beckons to me from the doorway
Of Congregation Zichron Moshe. "May I,"
He says to my companion, "borrow this
Jewish gentleman for a moment?" I follow
The man inside, down the carpeted aisle,
Where at the front, resplendent in
Polished wood and gold, stands
The as yet unopened Ark.

Now the doors slide back, an unfolded
Promissory note, and for a moment,
I stand as one among the necessary ten.
The braided cloth, the silver mounted
On the scrolls, even the green of the palm
Fronds placed about the room, such hope
Which breaks against my unbeliever's life.

So I ask, Nat, may I borrow you, for a moment,
To make a necessary two? Last time we lunched,
Enclaved in a deli, in the dim light, I saw
A bit of my father's face in yours. Not to make
Too much of it, but I know history
Stamps and restamps the Jew; our ways
Are rife with only momentary deliverance.
May I borrow you for a moment, Nat. We'll celebrate
By twos, the world's an Ark. We'll talk in slant
American accent to code the hidden language of the Word.

ACCIDENTAL MEETING WITH
AN ISRAELI POET

At the playground by the Con Ed plant,
this is strange: from tall brick stacks,
smoke is bleeding off into cloudless sky.
Little dreams, little visions must go like that.

Still, his boy and mine play in their soccer game,
each move, each kick or run precise and self-
contained. From one end of the field to the other

they go, from sun to deep shade. And there's no
poof, no gone, no fade into that all-capping blue.
Trampled ground, grass, sun-tinged webs of cable—

so this is how we reckon hope, as something
blotted up by matter that it might better
circulate in brick, in the squared-off shadows

of the power plant to commingle with children
and with games and sides, with wire and with steel
until, lo, the helmet of a soldier has sopped it up!
It sits there, insisting on a certain rightness.

And yet people's songs disperse into the air,
people's songs and rhetoric . . .

PALESTINE

Snow glides down in the West Forties.
Like a child, I could lick the snowflakes
from my wrists. In storms,
bums will nibble at the wood of tenement doorways.
The weather precipitates dreams, fantasies, I too
have my dreams of the snow's purity,
of its perfecting worlds, so little like my own.
Could I be a gentleman of this snow, my calling card
one evanescent flake to place upon a blemish?

Frankly, I'm delighted with a new scientific proof:
at any moment at least two places on the globe
must experience similar weather. Hence my
Palestine and hence my joy. Baudelaire
watched the Negress in the street stomp her feet
and imagine date palms. I don't want the territory,
just the intensity of a visit. *Sh'ma Yisrael*, only
the symbol world holds you and me or I and Thou.
Sh'ma Palestine, aren't you always where snow falls.

I I .

My Palestine, which means I love one woman,
so why not two? Which means I love that distant sky
and the lovely irritants of my inner eye. My tears
for what in life is missed. The Red Sea of my philosophy
will irrigate with salt these barren lands.

Does snow fall there too?

III.

Always somewhere else, and always held by someone else . . .
Sweet figs, sweet thighs to Suez or Port Said.
But when snow falls one's place is yet another place.

IV.

In that salty biblical sweetness, why avenge?
Grief is vectored north, east, west, the Wailing Wall.
Why avenge? Terror has cast its rigid mask,
and with fraternal semblance, transformed all
into sisters and brothers. Why avenge?
Only the dead wear human faces.

V.

Yea, though I am not lifted out of sorrow,
yea, though the opus of self-regard endoweth me
for nearly nothing, I have not forgotten snow. I
have no more forgotten snow than other poets forget
time or blackbirds. I have, with love, put the snow aside,
I have let the snow melt so that I may envision Judea
as a stately gentile lady, a crusader, a crusade.

VI.

I am so far away,
yet for Americans
distances are musical.
So I am near. I am with snow
which softens the city in which I live.
I am in the Forties and the snow glides down
and fills all the niches that lie between
the living and the dead.

MAMALOSHON

At night, dream sentences
That will not write themselves.

And there are phrases
You forget. Dawn comes;

It's only luck
Her breast is not your mother's.

So much touched by words,
At least you live.

What escapes makes for the grave—
A respectable marker.

CONSTELLATIONS OF WAKING

on the suicide of Walter Benjamin at the Franco-Spanish border, 1940

Something you wrote:
"Eternity is far more
the rustle of a dress

than an idea."
What odd sounds
to listen to

beneath occluded skies
that darken rivers,
Dneiper, Havel, Ebro,

murmuring contained
between
their tree-lined banks . . .

"In the fields
with which we are concerned,

knowledge comes only
in flashes. The text
is thunder rolling

long afterwards."
And thus, and thus . . .

*

These constellations,
which are not composed of stars
but the curls of shriveled leaves

by which the tree expressed
the notion of the storm. You
lived in storm, your outer life:

"adversities on all sides
which sometimes came
as wolves." Your father—

Europe was your father
who cast you on the path,
hungry, into constellated cities:

Berlin, Moscow, Paris.
Where would
Minerva's owl alight,

on what dark branch
to display its polished
talons?

*

1940
and in Paris, the library
is lost.

Books
no longer on the shelves—
how sweetly

they were "touched," you wrote
"by the mild boredom
of order."

*

Curled leaf,
one among many
on trees that lead

to a border crossing.
But black wolves in France,
they have changed the idea

of eternity. Toward
Port Bou, bright dust
mixing

with the ocean's salt air.
Wave-fleck from train:
each spun light

must have its meaning.
So to consider
as ultimate work

that sea bed of
all citation—
you'd allow nothing of your own—

thus the perfected volume.
No author?
And then no death?

The sea is inscribed
with *The Prayer*
for the Dead. No

author and then
no death? But the leaf
acquired shadow by

the ideal of light,
scattered light
the father

never recognizes.
The books are not
on shelves,

for that was Paris.
This the closed road
from Port Bou

which glistens with the dew
of morning. Redemptive
time

which crystallizes
as tree, as leaf
on the way to a border.

v

TWO SWANS IN A MEADOW BY THE SEA

High dunes falling away
To spongy ground, water lying
In brackish shallow pools
A few feet from the surf.

Broom and high grass hide
A dozen birds. They twitter.
We take it in as best we can,
The sea's sound, all
The marvelous growth.

No need to ask, to answer
How sky and hilly tufts,
Noise of cars on the road above

Are so composed to bring us,
Our eyes level with the sea,
To where two white forms
Rest their lovely necks
As though in self-caress,
Looking at each other.

A NIGHT FOR CHINESE POETS

Newcastle, Wyoming

All day, to have met with poets,
Bureaucrats, teachers, to be weary
Of one's own kind, of the numberless

Diamonds and snowflakes written in
Children's poems. Then at the motel
Where the running fountain builds an immense

Sea-anemone of glittering ice—the ducks
That forgot to go south quack around it—
I sit down to write you a letter, perhaps

A poem. And outside the moon turns the North Platte
Into frozen jade. Remember Li Shang-yin's jade
Pieced into a screen behind which she moved,

His love, his lucid madness. Now Orion's points
Are clear. The heavens bind at his girdle.
Wind glazes the puddles in the road,

Carries toward me the snow owl's shriek,
Thought and distance making hellish antipodes.
What now of the ink laden brush which "once

Forced the elements?" Weather beats at the window
Above the desk. I think of other Northern wastes,
A small boat tethered in an icy stream,

The exiled poet poised, regarding the paper's
Snowy white, "brooding on the uselessness
Of letters." *World, world*, invisible escort,

Messenger of the conjure-god, my bed's sweet
Ghost. I want to cry like one possessed
That this emptiness bears a shred-end of you
Into the room, that the heart is no less
For the page alone.

JANUARY NIGHTS

Sitting alone in a warm room.
Colors of brown, cream, gold.

My privacy extends to walls. I want
To exclaim that I am safe. Safe from what?

Beyond this is air, universe . . .
The lungs burn and the stars burn

With a suggested correspondence.
To imagine that I am just a nuance

Of what is happening, a trace
On the mandala of a poetry made

Out of the uncertain ache for certainty.
The paper's whiteness medicinally cool.

*

Light falls. Clouds pile as scud
Under the moon. In the west

A diffuse glow. Stopped traffic
And stars to be seen.

Only the lump ebony
Of the telephone

Outshines the night.
The moon looks iron.

Sister of cycles,
It pulls earth and tide,

Wave-tips of matter
Caught in repetitions.

Nearly mad with loneliness,
I rise, go to the window like many another.

*

The lights blaze in the great structures.
The air between, with swirls of snow, glows red.

Street, gutter, show tracks of a lone straggler.
Marks the wind will blow away.

But the sky is unstaunched. unswabbed
Of its endlessness: an angry blossom of love.

*

By the playground, the sky looks caged.
Moon shines amid patchy squares.

The swing creaks and the iron bars
Make a geometry.

Thoughts crowd of wanted toys.
Now, nothing as simple as that happiness

Nor the easy discard of broken things.
Pain is sharp—the space between us

Revealing realm upon realm
Of assailing glamour.

A WEEKEND OF SUN

What did I want to say? The building edge cut
bright blue air. Up Madison, a kind of favoring

light. Gauds of the world were there, glistening
gobs of silver swirled in tailored shrouds,

then doubled in backlit mirrors which gave us
back ourselves. We'd risen from sleep's

charnel ground to see our figures in the glass
beside the bracelet on its velvet pad, alone in *luxe*.

We laughed. I looked at your high cheekbones,
half buttoned blouse, dark studied contours.

I was the student of this theater, yet how to act my part?
Mind a cooled flame. Anticipation, the great, the absurd mentor.

The sun's corolla flared pride and sex;
the street's air was all magnetic storm.

I I

Downtown then, we joined the Soho crowds
in that odd net, the modern become medieval,

in throngs to which we all belonged. Grime
in pavement cracks, tattered posters

of the week's events, I wandered out, a tourist
of identities. I watched a man on high stilts

who played the people's grand buffoon. More laughter.
Story was dead, we agreed. Here was sun, obliterating

memory while we, like mathematicians, summed analogs
with gesture and with dress. Sat too and chatted.

Irony, giddy irony, an empryean of corrosive talk
as further away, on tall slabs of downtown stone,

sun fired glass. Up, up, the light burned
climbing that building, seeking for the roof.

As if to open the fire door at the top
and illumine the building's hollows.

Laughter which transmutes. In bar light,
mascara streaked. A face shocked into pain. Done.

I I I

Then through streets to the Square;
in the sunlight, each self an *auto da fé*

to burn on the regard of others—
bars and cafes our rehearsal halls,

our as yet unplayed dramas. More talk, dazzling
and accusatory, also brought more clarity.

Beside us, things we drank and ate: wine, cheese,
ashes smudged on cloth. We had added to the paraphernalia,

would make of common props an aesthetic
of the empirical, and we would see.

I V

That afternoon, to make love, to try to throw away
signpost, route, city map, direction, to enter

some unknowable. The light came as through a curtain
on a stage. That sun in the window exposed between us

an increment of space, a last blurred fortress of our holding.
We spoke of what was false but wanted true: ways of knowing

to become ways of celebration. We had become two words, two
parts stripped of meaning, sounding for each other only an echo.

LATE VISIT

And wasn't it the traffic of the world
we heard five flights up?
If it was street noise,
it was also more. The windows rattled,
our arms and legs rocked backward,
thrashed out a scripted pain-blocking lust.
Your words came fast, like the buzz
of an engraving on a shiny bone or tusk.

At the window,
where curtains blocked
a human-reminding light,
muffled wheel and shout,
the unheard, you said,
was a shroud. It played
itself amidst the dishes,
wire and antenna to the clouds
which moved so slowly past,
so slowly past,
as though the sky
had grown external skin:
an anti-music to the music of all things.

Only a recluse
could hear it, you said.
Unuttered it came with the light
between the cooing plaints:
"I too sought another, sought another . . ."

BEING AT EAST HAMPTON

I .

"The Hamptons are the playground of the artists."

From within the yard of the little house
I like to paint, on Fabriano or D'Arches,
Cars pulled in under low trees.

At one time I used a child's set of paints;
Now I squibb the tube's bright colors
Onto a palate made of plastic.

This preparation looks forbidding,
Even contemporary—the hand holding
The brush an already anxious object.

Miles from the city, the ancient subjects
Seem gifted and returned: sun, light,
Shrub, the shadow's play on the car's

Metallic sheen. Inapt machinery
Which cannot stand against an age.
Not modern in execution, my little

Pictures long for the hard surety
Of the classic. But my being here
Observing is both accident and intention

Blurring together like cars and trees,
Like any number of different natures
In the pigments and the washes.

11.

Perhaps you wouldn't like this place
With its petite talk of art,
Its dishonored hopes of wildness.

Here the gesture fails,
Is like the sky's immense expanse,
Something outside ourselves,
Irrelevant and almost comic.

As it turns out, this
Was no place to vaunt an independence.
Nothing here can stand alone,
Neither hope nor fear

Nor the isolate houses
On their spits of sand
In which the sea is heard

Reminding the occupants
That they are human.

I I I .

In the sun's glare, one scans
The bay side's waters. The blue above
Is lucid, pieced around the clouds,

Trees and houses in precise detail.
Where we take our dips,
A sheer boring fix of things

Even to the little knots
Of healthy looking middle-class families.
This freeze-frame of an illusion

Now a broken open social code
(good for all but the realist novelist).
Little one knows one's self,

One's time. Thus that scare of
Faint strangeness one late afternoon
When the fog rolled in upon our picnic;

On the island opposite,
Two mute swans we could have dreamed
Beat about each other
Like mad Japanese ghosts.

I V .

Bleep, bleep emits the antenna,
Beacon light across the bay.

Nights, the wind drops.
In the stillness, the mind

Suddenly a partisan of things.
To want to grip, to cleave to an image,
Read it as some self-secret text.

Meanwhile she moves into waves,
Sound of human noise enfolded
In the seas, in the watery zones.

A half-clear lightness
Extends to her body's depth,
Liquidity shading into dark.

Phantom of infiltration,
To whom or to what would you speak?

And the clouds gone as from the world,
The moon a mirror choked on dust.

V .

Again, the foam-tip dark of waves
Brings in on its curves
Images of living and of dying.

Not identity, but a visionary lesson
In the drama of the littoral.
And the birds come and go,

Are duly noted. I swear
We do not live on fixities,
Shells or stars which once discovered

Seem always with us. Do you remember,
These too, found amid
Those inland mountain tops?

Yet the sea . . . the sea does not strive
To emulate the granite.
You are here; no need to put this note

In a bottle in the breakers.
The sea is just . . . the sea a few feet away.
To give it that.

V I .

Today at the jetty, the wind
Lifts mother-of-pearl flakes
Off the beach.

One with a deep pink hue
Blows into a groove of stone.
In the pale light

It gleams: a gem set
In a cold setting. No sails
Cut the grey bay's foil.

The bird lime dribbles hard
On the ledges of the rock.
A tossed-up shell

Pierced by a gull's beak
Shrills curiously in the wind.
Another held in the hand

Repeats the ocean mutedly.
Apart, apart, yet to make of this
A blended music.

The tidal pools respiring
As the ocean rejoins itself.

THIS MANY-COLORED BRUSH WHICH ONCE FORCED THE ELEMENTS

to J.A. (among Chinese paintings of eight dynasties)

I

Under an open window, palace ladies
tune the eight-stringed lute,
the one I love gone off to visit
a solitary temple amid clearing peaks.

She travels where the religious ones go,
following in their train, the peevish monks,
the fishermen, desiring to be devout,
the old with their trembling toes on Nirvana's gate,

who plod dutifully into winter struck mountains,
to see the blossoming peonies of the snow delicate as the ladies of the court.

Here I sit, with other dazed creatures
not knowing how to seek, too dumb to go south.
They must nestle in this leafless grove,
for the mountainous winter landscape
contains at least one bird
flitting from tree to peak to stream,
all the while singing for some knickknack peddler
who's made his fist of silver at the court.

When the seasons wheel through the year again,
perhaps my turn will come.

I I

Last year, two love-struck kids,
we gawked under the red cliff,
gazed in wonder at anchored boats.

I could smell the whiff of buffalo and calf
a child had driven to be bathed.
"Samantabhadra" he was muttering
as if the inland sea were some
Lotus Sutra-covered altar.

Contemplate what an *arhat*
and his attendants might do,
traveling among streams and mountains,
listening to a bird on a tree serenade a cataract.

Soon, when you return, we will go
to compose poetry on a spring outing.
Possibly, you will make verse and paint
the twelve views of the landscape,
the full sail on the misty river.
(Last time you let me put in
the five dragons, the two thin lines
that render Shakyamuni coming down the mountains.)

I I I

When teachers are asked, we are told:
attend the water and moon Kuan-yin.
Bless deeply this place
for the river village is the fisherman's joy.
It flows from his full heart
into the sky like inked bamboo or a prunus
in the hidden moon's pale light.

Here, the nine horses and the nine songs
are as venerated as the treasured aspects
of the white robed Kuan-yin. Here the Buddha
converts the *bhikshus*.

Honor also the bamboo, the rock and the tall tree.
There is both devotion and leisure enough to spare.
"Merits are like having a hundred birds and three friends".
So say the nine elders of the mountain of fragrance.

I V

This haven of the peach blossom spring
reminds me of the river village in a rainstorm.
Squirrels cavort among the grapes as in
a landscape in the style of Ni Tsan.

You remember his album: the five leaves
of Shen Chou. Also, the one leaf
that looks like three of Wen Cheng's.

V

Much to understand.
I can not give up my need for understanding.
So gladness to the scholar who returns
with his crane in the boat,
says his farewell to the unknowable Sea
of the North at Hsun-yang.

Such farewells blend like notes
of the many stringed ch'in in a secluded valley.
Old cypress and rock in the jade field,
Emblematic of the mountains of Ch'ing Pien
which were as beautiful as the paintings
of the ancient masters:
cloudy peaks, landscape studies, companions
strolling, as we have done, in autumn hills.

The masters slyly ask, do you know the difference
between those mynah birds, old tree and rocks
and these mynah birds and rocks?

I will look for spring on the Min River
or in the shade of pines in a cloudy valley.

V I

Chrysanthemums float in ink!
The tall bamboo is posed with distant mountains
as though in a landscape
—in the color style of Ni Tsan!
—as in a portrait of An Ch'i!

The leaves fall,
but the titles of paintings remain.
I have lived long enough to know
that I am in love with figments,
thigh turns and orchid boats peeping shyly.

One thing I have learned from the sage:
"you cannot grasp even a moment".
But I at least remember
the titles of the paintings.

Words, leaves, the thick black turn of the brush.
I have thought of you while writing this,
of a conversation in storied autumn.

Yes, Han-shan and Shih-te are with us.
Voices as from a landscape with a waterfall.

WATER, HEADS, HAMPTONS

"the unbearableness of idyllic literature" —Canetti

My dear,
it is summer. Time to be out of time.
Let us read together the world's newspapers.

But the wind blows away the pages of the *Times*—
they rise, stretch full-length in the breeze like
any vacationer wanting a day in the sun, an even tan
to return with to a city, to proclaim "I too have been away."

Let us read. We can! Memory is our language. We are two
minds that lie athwart each other, two continental plates
with errant nationalities that articulate via subterranean grit.
In time, we will grind this world to powder, to be upraised
and bleached by processes of the seas.

But the wind blows. The surf ripples and slaps with the sough
of all the living and dead it has dissolved, and, with a great
respiratory suck, deposits on the beach what waves
must leave even as they take back what must be taken back.

Ah, you hear the anti-noise where gusts expose the sheet
of crumpled newsprint buried in the sand. What is written
is written. But we will lean close, intent, where
wind-blown grains pepper the page with faint pings.

*

It is one of those days when my will seems no more
than the will to conflate utter laziness with a poem
or with roiling sleepily in some good sex. Sleep,

O languorous sleep where I am forgetful of the misery
of history, my brutal West, a dozing prince
before which all gives way.
                    And summer
lightning at the sea's rim transforms the high
gorgeous blocks of clouds into a dance, a shadow-screen
of our imaginable gods: blue Buddha, Shiva of the knife,
Kali who follows footsteps in trackless sand, aerated Christ!

*

A weird pang of nameless joy. Look, a swimmer's head
is bobbing in the sea. And I point, my finger
like a sunbeam in a barrel. Here's this head

that moves from horizon to beach, this flesh-dot
that seems to swim away from the end
of an entrapping sentence, re-opening its syntax,

and so, for once, is at work against
premature closure. So I identify
a brother eidolon against the tide's flat reach.

*

Summer's paradise. Its rhythm. But not
the incessant flights of midges swarming in dark air,
alighting on the body through which hope and pain trickle,
those substantial rivers flowing to the seas.

Will you swat the tic of memory and enter into
ever-present babble of flies? Madness of the words.
Old tropes like brilliance of coral shoals on which
waves break and shipwrecks and glittery cabin lights
are extinguished in the deeps.

*

To the white sands who will speak a name?
The quiet of dusk comes back. Noiseless flight
of gulls inscribes the air and the world goes down
in a rhythm of deepening colors.

Surely the gods we invent bring out the night's phenomena:
flux into perfection, corollas and auroras, St. Elmo's fire
for all those who suffer the agonies of speech.

                    Objects, you
no longer offer up yourselves for ceaseless dictation,
no language anyway, our mouths are on each other.
Some lord of silence rises with stars and planets . . .

V I

IN THE MOUNTAINS,
LINES OF CHINESE POETRY:

> *"the thread in the hand of a kind mother*
> *is the coat on a wanderer's back"*

Before she left this world, she stitched him tight.
Today, this mountain trail's her thread, on, up and out
to endless blue, and yet there's something unrelieved
about the space, his past, his childhood is
landscaped too. His fear for her, her damaged heart.

She slept on a throne-like bed at room's end
where he and his sister were not allowed to go.
He couldn't touch her, but, from where they stood,
he'd watch her sew. She was the view, but he was in it too.

Now his thoughts of her are like the bannered clouds
that float across the alpine grass, insubstantial
before the mountain's rock, hard otherworldly fact.
He would dream her back? Was she to inhabit every fear

and every wish? Eye-tug in mountain mist, he hoped,
in vacant, windblown heights, he'd find, not her, himself.
But it was only one improving stitch. She'd basted him, braided
thread right through his retina, her way itself defining sight.

BORN IN WATER

Born in water. I was born in
my mother's water and washed out
into the world from the burst sac.

When my mother died, we respected her wishes,
collected her ashes at the crematorium,
then spread them on the grass over my father's grave.

And because the wind was blowing,
we poured water from a plastic pitcher,
and added water from our eyes
so the ashes wouldn't blow away
but seep into the ground.

Mother and father, as on the day
I was conceived, mingled together.

PARTITIONS

The War

Lights out. The blackout curtains
Pushed aside. The moon was rising
Over hacked-off stumps of trees,

Limbs sawed away in the war's
Third year when the caterpillars
Came and went. We were sheltered

In our rooms, thrilled by the moon
Sailing down the river of backyards,
Over the chunky stumps, over roofs,

Chimney stacks and pots like sentinels
Against the star filled night. Safe,
Safe for the moment,

The air of conflict,
A small boy's war on stoops.
Yet even then, neighbors were gone;

Flags hung behind glass. My father,
Just returned from an army camp,
Looked in, then went to my mother.

Out the window, stars too were distinct.
And suddenly, night was the greater heart
Vibrating knowledge not of death

But of loneliness: desire itself
To never again be fully quenched.

The Oath

> *"the vow/that makes a nation one body not be broken"* —Robert Duncan

Was it only a few years ago
To have heard organ tones
Enlarge the fierce sad pomp?

Or was it when young. The weight
Of flag and anthem, *E pluribus unum,*
The nation upraised as god.

In the classroom, aged nine or ten,
Feeling aloneness, he had sung it,
"My country 'tis of thee . . ." he had sung

For apartness of his own,
A thrall which moved him
Toward company with others.

Yet why did he not hear the angry
Purpose, for which the falsehoods,
The fictions and tyrannies of war:

Parent coupled to the world,
The god-eye in that form,
Song set to receive it.

Was he not once the figure behind
Who longed and who ached,
Who did not know he moved in the falseness . . .

He could sing now on that theme
And find release. He could sing again
Inside.

He would hear first the childhood
And then the mockery, which entwined
As he thought the song must, gathering

So much for fear, so little
For love. Was this not the meaning
Of the note known for its own sake,

Was knowledge of the myth?

To hear the binding in which he stood,
Could stand so among the others
Who also sang:

In anthem once conjoined
The isolate man the child thought he was.

Street

Years later he would wake
As from a dream: had he
Grasped the elemental link?

The brownstone stoop
Piled against the brownstone house,
The way lives leaned on each other.

The horse-drawn cart
Was turning the corner
With its load of ice.

He followed with his mother
Watching the street weave and twist
In the great clear dripping blocks.

O how he wanted to let her hand go
And leap for chips and flakes
When the ice pick struck, sending

Fault lines through
That mad bent imagery.

3 A.M., The Muse

Not the power of speech
Nor the note blown into wholeness.
We seemed never to converse in the now as now.

What poetry there is
Is always late. Strange merely
To have thought. What

Rises out of what? Almost nothing
But this severe calm of identity.
I remember the animal moans:

The mute of that neighborhood
Of dusty laurels whom you released
From the locked up movie house

Down the block. Young, beautiful.
Her cries startling us in the summer
Night. She had fallen asleep,

Only woke when the show ended
And the screen had gone dark for awhile.

MIAMI WATERS

Closing Up His Office Near The Ocean

Across the street
The bank clock winks *our* time
And the flat slabbed glass of walls
Catches knotted twists of light
Reflected off the ocean's waves
A few streets away.
     Tossed in a black
Plastic trash bag: correspondence,
Scraps of old account books, stubs
Of receipts and checks.
     Meanwhile, the sea
Recycles itself, holds what
Gives it its brackishness: the salt,
The inert, the living, the dead, swaying
In the one permeating taste.
     In the office, not everything
Is thrown away. Brought back to the house
Will be photos and mementos, separated out
To supply the measured adequacy, the sharp flavor
Of earned sense. The rest could as well be left
Scattered on desk or floor
For the cleaning man to be puzzled by,
To pick over: some item overlooked,
A blank never filled, gain or loss,
Knowledge of which would end
In profit.
     Now the mouth
Of the bag shows almost full.
Tied with a wire twist, it will gleam,
Black lump—not secrets but *minutiae*—
Under the florescent light
Like an unused altar in a corner.

At Biscayne Bay

Again, this year,
Palms suffer blight

But the luxurious green
Is elsewhere apparent

We take rides in rented cars.
Places you no longer visit,
Places fitfully recalled.

There's little looking and no talk.
Memories only intensify this sense
Of withering amidst profusion.

At last, we come to the bayside.
The paving runs into high grass

And the trees reach out, above
Where we used to fish. Dazzling

Underneath in sunlight and shade,
The current's one ineluctable:

Its constant change.

Aftermath

Waking to the sound of rain
In your house, almost a stranger's house,

I was reminded of years ago when
The storm's eye passed over the city

And left a violent harvest on the beach.
We kids went out, picked our way

Over fallen power lines, snapped trunks
Of trees, tongues of sand which reached up

Streets to cars and houses. Under grey skies
We marched gaily, survivors, to the ocean

Where among the bloated fish I found
A treasure, an ancient alarm clock propped

On sand. We played with it as in some dream
While offshore, the boats sprung loose

From their moorings tossed among the waves,
Spar and wreckage taking up the same wild motion.

St. Francis Hospital

A noise down the hall,
Another old man howls: "this is not my son,
This is not my daughter."

In the room, your eyes are wide,
Alert to what you think beyond you.

With part of you not here
(and not knowing where) we talk,
But conversation's not the proper word.

Someone has thoughtfully turned
The TV on above the bed,
The volume down.

It plays for benefit
Of nurse or visitor
Who at certain times must turn away.

In your head,
A Sybil rages,
Implodes together places, times and years—

A text unbearable in its modernity.

Perhaps the world,
Which does not cohere in the world,
Coheres in one self, in one rememberer.

I think you want to tell me
One last time
That this is something shared

But your thoughts come almost
As another language. In the night
Outside, the arc lamps burn

And under the bridge the canal
Runs light and dark. The palms gleam
Like silvery feathers. I try to follow

Into the spillway of your words,
Meanings as loose upon the world
As this powdery effect of the light's particles.

FATHER STUDIES

Bindweed

Looking back to see you clear

The unkempt green clinging to the brick
You, framed against its swirls
There, in a sense, forever

How gripped in the child's equity
Equity of a weed and its twine
Toward flower

And the child, that delicate
Respectable bud

Following the light's trope
Bush, wall, petal, bug . . .
Not yet marking out a way of judging.

Prophecy

You too were born
Of a time and place

And now in the grey light
You sit avoiding blame

—All that you did not do
For yourself—

Avoiding what the flesh
Still wants to tell you

Complicity, complicity
Of reason gone to blame

As though we were all born
Owing blame, and whatever we did
Would barely change the story

"If you could see what I can see!"
I used to shout in my fear

When the light behind the blinds
Was like a seep of time

A millennium of light
Caught in the baffles

History

Such power you once had
To comfort and to hold

And now to find you
Weaker than myself

By that, think I wield
The power of your happiness

But promise and promise
Have gone to defeat

And the last defeat
Is unimaginable

The ghosts
Scattered now upon your eyes
Look back, *not out*

They emit a soundless howl
As they join
The century's conspirings

Whole Cloth

Slats pulled, light blocked
Caught in whorls of random pattern

I know the sun blazes on the windows
At the room's far end

You sit upon the bed's edge
Shrunken, coiled over, as before
The altar of a vengeful god

And even now, the voice cracks
Remembering the vial's squeak
Upon the glass

Fear, and love which would save,
Complete the fabric

Emergency's Furrow

Sick, and the life narrowing
The road too clear ahead

Lost inside yourself, huddled
In an old striped robe, a tattered Joseph

I don't wonder that you commune
With the living and with the dead
—all are now your brothers

When

When you were not there
I used to talk to the stuffed bear,
The wide-eyed doll

Their secret lives
I matched, adventure for adventure

Now all dreams become entwined
Terror with love, yours
With mine

Is this not the instruction:
The true life at last in the weave
Taking up the thread

THROUGH THE BINOCULARS

"are the cranes returning to you" —Hölderlin

I .

White egret plumed against green grass
Great blue heron, these the first two
Noticed this year at the Point.

Heads dart under rushes for bright small fish,
For shells succulent with flesh: the movement
Of their beaks eats up and transposes time.

Air gusts off nearby flats. A moist wind
Carries the rot of split open shells; death
Scent and harbor scent, and the water's wide curl

Dark at the edge. And the wind tugs
Shadows at the birds' feet; sunlight
Scintillates and mazes at the lens.

This Mnemosyne loves: what distorts her weave
What the weave distorts in time.
And the bird book too

Is almost an advisory: there are herons
That fail to migrate, remain in the North
When winter comes and fall victims to severe weather.

And wasn't it only last week to have read
From the Chinese of the warrior who falls,
Who does not change, who has failed to submit

To the passage of the seasons. This summer,
Sic transit, my father has passed by. Overhead
A paper kite, a wind bell's tinkle, and to think

An ear less to hear. Isn't this 'made up,'
That the father who has died has migrated.
Isn't this a changing of the season?

I I .

Reeds shift in the wind, first gold
Then a dry silvery grey. Actually
The color they are cannot be grasped.

And the water throwing back its blue
Deepens shadows. What false power
Tries to posit two: observer and observed.

Something I observed is gone
And no ritual to perform
But a kind of letting go.

Thick rush of water
At the harbor's mouth; surely, it looked
This way last year. Yet I'm told

Unseen currents reclaim the old channels.
The heron dips its graceful head, claims
The fingerling in the time-frame of the day.

I I I .

The day which also frames thoughts of cars
And people. That she borrowed the car,
Had trouble with the door, and the latch

Won't close, and by the tracks the car will sit
Unsecured. Years ago I moved away,
Had trouble with the locks. Yet this

Is less about what is taken or escapes,
Or even that the dead can't talk or have left.
This is only to say the dead will have released
All they will release.

I V .

Some herons remain beyond their time.
Some bright tasty thing at the water's edge
Overrides the migratory mechanism.

Bright things have claimed my new wife's time,
Have claimed mine as well. We tried in our times
To reclaim a season.

V .

A story: to send a letter
To his father dead in the pure land
Of Shambhala. The son looks first

To the sun and the moon. Their light
Reaches, but they cannot deliver the letter.
He spies clouds passing lightly by, thinks

They can go there, but can they carry
The message? Birds fly overhead, going north;
These he appeals to without success. No one
But himself can deliver the message.

V I .

"are the cranes returning to you?"
Long lines fitted to elegies, strange hope
In constant repetition of word and phrase.

Or stand here. Binoculars make of the world
An eerie visitation.: not only enlargement
But the coated len's spectral hue. Odor of

Salt and sea pine, astringent as ancient myrtle.
How do you come to be here? With the twentieth
Century at your back. How does one lose the sense
Of the hymnic and must sing only of what is past.

V I I .

In "harbinger" I heard the word "harbor" sound,
Found they both stem off an old French root . . .

As through the telescoping glass, a steady
Surface grain shows change: black-flecked rot
Of new leaf blight, the bleached red edge

Like a portent of the Fall. Look close.
New yellows can be confused with autumnal tones:
Harbingers. So that even the terms for seasons

Are a kind of babble. You can hear such confusion
In the language of the fathers as they fall
Through time. It sounds like hope haunting

The epochal voices which seek a stay against
Their time. *O keep me from this death*. Father,
All your words have died, yet, curiously, their muses

Live on. They hide here, in shadow
Between house and ground, or huddled by
The staved-in boat or by the day-lily's stalk—

Wherever these birds gather and animate
What I write, telling me death too
Can be enlivened. The ear is a crypt.

VIII.

Of another poet. That the bird's feathers
"dangle down." Do you remember that phrase
From a time just past? Dead world. Dead poets.

I know someone who never met him
But called him father. Is there
Some residue to carry with this thought?

IX.

The breast of the heron close up
Is a maze of gnats. But think of the plumage
Of the dead. "*Tallis*, fresh underwear, black socks,

Bring these," scribbled on the funeral parlor envelope.

X.

You were here long after your time, here
And unable to care for yourself, unable
To talk, to know who had come into the room,

To remember what was said. How to keep such
Thoughts, which only a god or a presence
Is entitled to forget?

The mother, memory, has seen this cycle,
How the birds come back, how
The dead leaves are the new leaves' bed.

X I .

Look at the heron's feathers
Almost a shimmer in the wind or watch
Its nervous eye circuiting.

This is memory, this the message.

It is said the warrior's eyes ought to be sharp.
Perhaps he can foresee the onset of the seasons.
With binoculars, one sees further than one might.

X I I .

Beautiful the world the dead have left us to see.
Beautiful the shell, thin and delicate in its own right,
Yet beautiful as a beautiful woman. Beautiful

The other isles where you lived and where the dead
Also go from, where palms fan out against the wind
And cruise ships studded with lights make way

Toward the sea, and the pelicans and gulls denied
To the dead follow behind. Beautiful this thought
Of the dead, the memory of the dead that follows

Like the waters out to the sea.
Is there some residue for the new season?

ON DRY LAKES TRAIL

Mother and father gone, and I, the new orphan,
new to my orphan-ness, summon what I can
to staunch the little gap.

For these rounds of my grief, I imported fauna
into the poem. For father, who died first,
the heron was imploded into lines and stanzas.
I thought of white-feathered Chinese death
and tic-like nervous beauty. So many times,
in his last years I saw him with his fingers
worrying his lower lip.

Mother, I played on reversals, the facts
of your life. You'd been cut by a dozen
operations, both breasts gone. And when,
by accident I found insurance photos
in an envelope amid the memorabilia,
I saw how the surgeon's knife had given
you the body of a male.

O miracle, that the force of you survived.
I saw it in that Bighorn ram at 12,000 feet
just above the Dry Lakes Trail, who pawed
and pawed at his succulent piece of turf,
flashed white battle scars in the brown fur
of his sides. I sensed the great warp
of distance by which you had to protect yourself.

High, high, high the reminders take me,
first against the sky, Horn Peak
to the right, Jane's photograph
catching you all silhouette, back-lit
and black, authority and severity
flowing from you into horned isolate strength,
bone and space twisted on itself.
Yes, that was your grass, and it was we
who left, stumbling down the slope,
down to the trees and air, warmer air,

down to the path. But I hung back, Mother,
because of tears, hung back, as did you,
I walked home alone.

IN ELEGIACS, BIRDS OF FLORIDA

GULLS

Mother, those last vistas: you perched in the apartment which overlooked the wrinkled bay and the city whose patterned lights on the far shore resembled constellations. Near death, the whole world became a reading. So you too, father. At the home, I watched with you the palm fronds wave idly outside your room. Your eyes seemed to follow shadows on the walls, mind traceries, glints and powder darks, fan waverings of now and past, sea anemone, coral branch, yielding design but inarticulate.

Short stroll between you two, about the distance gulls will leave around a solitary walker who, at sunset, skirts the water's edge. A step too close either way and a gull will fly off, then another and another, to bob offshore on black water. Always a further horizon to inscribe a dividing line, a last blaze way out that catches the surf's turned edge. Before the salt nest of tombs, this consolation.

FLAMINGOS

Are nearly a secret. Half gawk, half grace, their thin legs hold them unsteadily erect. They teeter on non-being. A flock, they move as one outlandish pink-feathered thought. Something like the mind's repository of hosts and legends, their passage through the world, the double helix's cosmic joke: herd, family, tribe—how dead shades in groups are driven across the universe.

SNOWY EGRETS AND HERONS

Are ubiquitous. They fish in the inland canals behind the great hotels or at bayside, near backyards and docks of pale white homes. I have seen them hang silently in trees, eye's gift, sacs of tissue-papered fruit, the kind one buys for funerals. At sunset, they march their young across the highways and the Tamiami Trail, their nests in sleepy willows and cypress. With the beat of their wings, they have made the Everglades the other side of Lethe. They roost too beside the airport, calm and self-involved, standing at runway's end in shallow puddles amidst their own reflections.

MIND BIRDS

With my son, sitting in the park in Miami after a trip to the Parrot Jungle, we conjured up invented birds: the Guantanamo Guano Dropping Bat, the Elixir Eider whose feathers could stuff waterbeds, the Woid Boid, the Brooklyn poet's finest fowl.

I imagine, too, the Memory Bird—O synapse that can scribe its following arc! It circles over these peopled beaches of Hades and Limbo like the fabulous Garuda, a bird which never lands nor rests. Such a creature is too expensive to feed or tame or bring to earth to lay its unblemished egg of certainty. Still, at its highest flights, its claws tear at one's heart and liver more viciously than the eagles of Prometheus.

WORDFLOW

(1997)

LECTURE WITH CELAN

How many know
the number of creatures is endless?

So many know,
only a gasp in their questions is possible.

All that fullness—
of wounds that *won't scar over,*

pain's grillework
persisting in the memory.

What sets one free
within the sign and blesses the wordflow

without barrier?
Not literature, which is only for those

at home in the world
while air is trapped in the sealed vessel,

contained in our
containment, our relation to earth.

Omnivore language,
syntax of the real, riddling over matter,

more difficult to ken
than the talmudic *angelus.* Thus what black

butterflies of grief
at this leaf, at this flower? Already you

have moved over ground
beyond past and future, into a strange *voiceless*ness

close to speech,
both dreadful and prophetic—all else utility

and failure. And now,
the work builds to a word's confines,

to a resemblance of lives
touching the history of a rhyme between earth and dying.

LEAVING THE MUSEUM

What dark did you want, of many?
The line on the page, Baudelaire's hand

at self-portraiture, cross-hatched
skull, flab of the cheek in light.

But also the splash of an ink wash—
an inverted halo clouding that face

given only to prescient
melancholy . . . What dark did you want?

The runnel of the walkway
between Maillol's immense recumbent

goddess and a Duchamp constructed
of canisters and planes teaching

an oblivion, while another dark,
cupping the one you've studied,

is taking up time differently,
opening the great heart of the city

to the lamb, until passing from
the galleries to the streets, it claims

itself to be a lost armature of the universe.

This dark, cupping the darkness
you studied, is the ink mottling water,

fog around streetlamps,
stone and traffic's murmur.

MICHAEL HELLER . 341

STANZAS AT MARESFIELD GARDENS

Freud's house in London, now a museum

The dream manifest as ruin. He feared forgeries
and eliminated suspicious items from the collection.

Still, after his death, many fakes were discovered.
The ruin manifest as dream. He deployed figurines

of ancient deities at which he gazed. Those with
half-turned heads he positioned over journals.

*

His antiquities: the Buddhas, the protectors,
the instructive voids he saw in Roman jars

half-filled with a crematorium's ash and bone.
Those heaps! Their inimitable deserted air—

out of that clay and back to clay, *adamah!*
What to will from these shapeless mentors of speech?

What utterance lifting powdery blackened grains
to something human? What voice to throw out

against those other gods always in miniature in their cruel
presiding, in their fixed vesseling in bronze and stone?

Time-maimed fickle Isis-Osiris, noble Avalokitesvara
whose raised hand is a gesture to the named and unnamed

who stand guard over the scriptor. And there too,
are the onyx-faced ones, scowling at heresy and betrayal.

Do not look askance; do not miswrite! Thus, to hear
each *persona* in the room utter form, in babbled hope

of words poured back over the eons, in hope of words
given to gods as sacrifice, as exigent futures

of sound, divinities claimed in flawed obeisances.

*

The collection was a dream unmarred by forgeries
he ruthlessly eliminated. Manifestations of half-turned heads

he thought of as ancient deployments, listening to patients
as though gazing on collections of ruined forgeries.

He deemed these manifestations as collections he deployed.
Half-turned dreams of patients gazing toward ruins,

of ancient figurines he looked at ruthlessly while journals
under deities lay open manifesting as his collections.

WITHOUT OZYMANDIAS

Time, ruins, knowledge . . .

the traveler was fortunate.

*

Who finds the pedestal
finds the poem.

*

Ink and effacement

—only companions
of last things owned

Sand has its texts,
mica and feldspar,
stars and nestled bones

to write you to your shadow

*

High dunes, wind rolled
to long curvilinear trenches

amidst the tides of erasures,
an entombment of display cases—

fulgurites collected after lightning storms

beaded quartz, dry curlicues—

granules adhering to fire-drawn surfaces
mineraled, glassine, acolytes

fused to unwarrantable blackness

*

What tribes to wander with Moses?

*

Sere alchemy
that Jesus disappeared
in the numbered
days of an older Flood

A tempted St. Anthony
at the ledge

so a bush burns,
the mirage shimmers

an extraordinary
absence of mirrors

solitude of the grain

to notice one's own aloneness.

*

Why to remember the trepanned
and bleached skull of the angel?

the angel which has none of my earthly wants

who to remember semblances of desiring
as pale and colorless?

To place a word on it,
like a bit of mica winking in sun

—no god to forget
the foresworn babel—

to place time on it,
as though time were
handwriting . . .

*

Fortunate traveler.

AT THE MUSE'S TOMB

AFTER READING

The long eerie sentences were fates as the savannahs of Georgia and the Carolinas were endless stanzas in pine and swamp water.

Searches were made among the word-habitats that mattered, consonances of landscapes and self, half-geographies contoured from remembrances, shadowed and opaque.

The rest, the unexplained, the transparency, the mirrors and the dust, were to be talked away as dreaming.

The investigation missed horror.

Yet no one complained, preferring to imagine a pale language, paler than a linen tablecloth or the desert's unlit night.

Poe's white Baltimore stoop mounting to a door.

FORM

Nothing to ennoble the passion for measure and number, for the hard precincts of form, that uncanny love, surely as indictable as any great crime or gratuitous enormity.

Yet, with one's attention span, the mind wandered out, a weighted thing to be pushed forth on a cloud of moistened breath, to soar and curl itself about a street or a city.

Hungerings occurred amid the silted isobars of hope, in love's calms and tempests, sloughs of logic gone astray which had left us open to chance and to a desiring to persist.

The self's tellings were another moon haunting its own sublunary. It sought itself as a name high over soil it had made, rocks, cities, isolate worded beings.

MNEMOSYNE

O Mother memory, yes!

I had visited in Spain, did my Goya-walk to the *n*th, but it barely got me to Lorca.

The *duende*, mysterious visitor, came and went.

The dead war ravaged among villagers.

And suddenly the muse was no longer a headstone stippled with *palabras*.

THE LOCAL

Actually, by accident of birth, I was born to homelessness and nothingness.

Later I opted for the local, for the 63rd A. D. election district and its bands of refugees who vanguard at the doors to ATMs.

Also to what the city advertises, gunk or hair-gel, the stickiness of lost meanings, of signs secured by ripped awnings, foreclosures on the dark, dry pavings of a night skittish with deaths.

Beyond words' portals, I was always turned back, a bewildered Orpheus, city gentleman to Eurydice, an Amphion who gathered up stones into another hell-heap.

And now I feel a bit sickness-haunted, peering at the ineffable from an alley.

OUR TIME

Media voices over-wash all, blurring the inevitable: Psyche's credit-card sorting of the selves into collectives.

From the great engarblement, words are lifted out, and, in the current lexicon, crowd aside columns of pictures, taking one past new literals for contemplation among metonyms of blank.

GHOST

I was thinking about memory again, writing its letter home.

Before she died, her face, her favorite objects, etc.

Breakfasts were sweet, even . . .

On the table, the plunged gold plate of the bell on a silver creamer.

Someone left a world in it, a layer of puddled whiteness
resembling a page, viscous, absorbent, richer than the *néant*
Mallarmé inscribed on.

NEVER ONE

Because it is almost sound, it was meant for sharing.

We watched together the sun pour in the window,
motes of light on glass and wood.

Who was home to this homeless light?

Together we dreamt of transports, of residences as glints off mica-ed rocks,
centerless sheens bouncing from the frozen lake.

One felt the very slightness of being, almost validity's dusting up.

Yet also love, which hid us from the fiction's glare.

Pointless to ask for the addressee of desire.

Or that the mind misspoke its sonic phantoms and conjured the self which erred and brought us to this place.

A P H A S I A

And now, the demiurge possesses a lightness, a wet nuzzling of hope blind to the part played by the geometer's art.

Bleached one, O muse, I think of you, your silences where the throat catches on emptiness, *that free flight into the wordless.*

O teacher, the sky's light is fading, and I have sought that one place, speechless to the moon, an omen blossoming at its own edge, a bizarre portraiture in the rush of things portentous.

Bleached one, what was strategy?

What was truth?

The plangent lucidity, the glass through which the light flowed.

IN PARIS

The Place de la République's outdoor cafe, white wine
in a glass so thin it blurs realms with the greenery,

and with a statue patina-ed bronze, its plaque too far to read,
dull-lettered, pigeon-marked, possibly a thesis on history.

Yet the student lesson for today was the bomb at Boulevard
St. Michel, and the tourist's heightened sense increased

in the evening's Semtex blast near Le Drugstore at L'Étoile.
Luxe, voluptuousness, the children of freedom have returned.

Benjamin was here in the late 1930s, jackboots down the street,
wrote to Scholem of his "estrangement from everyone he knew."

Old Paris, carnage and death, St. Denis grilled on the *champs*,
the slaughtered diners at Goldenberg's in the Marais. I have

eaten there too, and now the wine's tincture puckers the lips,
and then the buds of flavor burst coming through, like a life

passed from one into another's care, in the City of Light
where hope was stifled once between *le mot juste* and *le mot juif.*

PRONY'S CALCULATIONS

O new Magnificat, in this world to live *à la Philosophie*!
This was the banner hung in the nave where the singer would sing

Reason's dithyramb and stave. Came *Brumaire*, Prony computed
his endless tables, a rigorous dream splayed across the page

to the fifteenth decimal reminding one who lived that while
he ate and consumed, numbers writhed in the mind's temple.

O serpents of days which had no use for you, save to time you
to oil the blade's drop, and to bewilder you enough

to be pacified by marks the sea scours on nature's mysterious cockle shell.
Prony named them all with a digit until, *citoyens*,

thought was not reverie. The dead god of ourselves was enclosed
in a tomb with no place to think of the incalculable, which waits

upon a futurity of hopes and arrives upon flesh as pain,
rooming like a ruined aristocrat in memory's chateau.

THINKING OF MARY

In memoriam, M.O. d. 1990

On the ride down to Carmel, as we talked,
the held back feelings surged like the Pacific,
and suddenly a young girl's face broke surface.

I was seeing fifty years back, swerving
with the roadway into old stories:
the barge canals of France, Pound and Rezi,

time's acoustics on an odd headland like this,
sounding a way to the end of the century.
Then we left the car and walked on hilltops,

the bay spread off West, and to the East,
the Sierra's bluish haze. Your painter's eye
picked out the sights, weighing and measuring

the dry California light, the brown wiry grasses
ruffling. Later at Marie's, the tick of the pines
mingled with house talk: poems, art, Jeffers' Tor,

the harsh look you shot at those you'd barely suffer,
these were as balks for you against the age. The woods
outside were a paradise to the imperfect, the branches

fanning into windstreams. And that you judged—
frightening those near you—a sharpened knife to pare
out Mary, *not* the poet's wife. After George's death,

it struck me, you came into your own in your collages,
piecing sky blue paper onto cloth until they belled out
with the continent's inhuman spaces. You moved from

the bedroom shared with him into a smaller space, futon
on the floor, as though recalibrating yourself. Perhaps
you were listening there for the new life growing, growing

back like a circle on itself or like the ocean's recurrent tidal sweeps,
scouring the present for the past until you were a child
again before loss and could begin at last your weeping.

PARENTS' GRAVE

To learn from what you do there,
under a mound, not even a mound
but the barely perceptible
rise in the earth.

To learn your now famished learning,
that the texts were no good for you,
the hand in its doings, the head full of play,
comic, but leaving the hunger you must leave.

All you hoped to accomplish by now.
And I put my head down to that ground, still
a child, instructed by what only you can teach,
a piece of the night fallen into it.

The old machine, time and place, where I put you both.
Tears which come. The new language, only translation.

ONE DAY, WHAT YOU SAID
TO YOURSELF

Winter. Two trees in the yard of Friends Seminary
are without leaves, stark in their denudement.

The world glazed with cold, the homeless argue
in the park, their angry voices leaving them more naked.

The trees, the limbs of which held foliage, branch
and twig that winter freed, ride higher and higher,

angling into the sky and sun. But you had tired of
the bare data, the nictating perception which crowed

like a bird, *I live*, exuding the old lyric order of the world,
so that a corner was turned, the image bedded in stealth,

to emerge neither for nor against. Only some principle
you wanted without war or hope for life better than

a privileged fold in history such as the powerful make, rather
something just there in the interstices, call it a moment,

the fragment, the sweet taste of her in the second
person, for the record, later the ambush. You

encountered the trees and the trees met you and won.

S H E

is looking up, and then she is not looking up.
With a lovely uncontrollable quiver, she's become herself.

I can see she is no longer the breasts which offer up
their enticements, nor the dark mysteries of the pubis.

She is not even her laugh. She is she, without residuals.
'*Bye, my love*, I think. And, possibly, *by* my love? And I

am happy, happier even than when her mouth is on me and I
gasp at the ceiling.

TO POSTMODERNITY

Some of the poets have discovered
that we are anxious to disconnect
the dots and words, to invoke
speech's possible ramble
coming in, awash and surrounding
like a tide, like a tide
of dead leaves whispering
our autumnal contingencies.

And true, the clichés abound,
exposing our non-being
and the certain emptiness of death,
the passivity needed to survive
the modern by luxuriant asides.

And yet love's obliquity
is still a language,
a tutoring mastery of desires
and hurts, leaps and kneelings
at the utterance of a name.

CLASSICAL THEME

To the morning traceries are ascribed hope and promise of a day
whereby an intellection is erased from the ordinariness of truth.
The mind secures, in semblances, the yellowed clouds, thinner
and whiter toward the West, those legibilities consonant

with a self always imagined, always beyond reach. And so the sky is sown
    with futurities, omniscient scatterings, thought's

anointments. We are the impossibles of these wants, unloosing
our grasp so that, briefly, the hope of love may leave a mark.

As in waking with her from sweetness, a memory of completeness becomes
    an enabling myth, and one awaits the requisite fears

which fuel our constant devolutions, the gorgeous realm abiding.

SAG HARBOR, WHITMAN, AS IF AN ODE

I

And so again, to want to speak—as though floating on this world—
thoughts of Sagaponak, of Paumanok, "its shore gray and rustling,"

To remember late sun burnishing with a pale gold film
the feathery ghosts of blue heron and tern, of that same light

furrowed in the glyphed tracks to bay water. And at night,
to scrape one's own marks in sand, a bio-luminescence underfoot

by which we playfully signaled, as the heat of bodies also
was a signal to turn to each other in the guest house buried

in deep sunk must and trellised scents. As though, again, to be
as with mossed graves which, even as they lie under new buds,

are worn and lichened, chiseled over with letter and number,
entrapped, as in the scripts of museum words, *trypots* and *scrims*.

And so, like whalers, whose diaries record a lostness to the world
in the sea's waves, to find ourselves in talk's labyrinth where

the new is almost jargon, and we speak of lintels of a house
restored or of gods who stage their return at new leaf or where

pollen floats on water in iridescent sheens.

I I

But also now, to sense mind harrowed in defeats of language,
Bosnia, Rwanda, wherever human speech goes under a knife.

And to be unable to look to the sea, as to some watery possibility
which would break down the hellish rock of history that rides

above wave height as above time. Strange then, these littorals
teeming with sea life, with crab and ocean swallow. Strange then,

to walk and to name—glad of that momentary affluence.
And so to find again the vibratory spring that beats against

old voicings, old silences, this waking to those fables where
new bees fly up, birthed spontaneously from the log's hollow,

to hear again the latinate of returning birds keeping alive
curiosity and memory, as if the ear were to carry us across hope's

boundary, remembering the words: *Now, I will do nothing but listen!*

EXIGENT FUTURES

(2003)

CYCLICAL

> *It was on that day when the Names were not,*
> *Nor any sign of existence endowed with name.*
> —Divani Shamsi Tabriz

I.

I was remembering how the city took shape by the offices of light. How our words were lovely evensong, trilling above the muted rumble of buses, delicate, yielding, a kind of looseness twanging off the metallic forest of rooftops.

We had wormed ourselves down into darkness, descending, self-blinded air-moles, and then sun and memory rose, and our plangent mindfulness was godlike, a backing and filling which laid out the boulevards and crushed the sparrow.

At midday, a precision of shadows illumined the telltale refuse in the streets.

Love hectored: were we to exist, our *being* a kind of coruscation across the sallow air?

(So many machines, so much impelled movement. It was left to verbal mechanisms to draw down the power, to blow fuses, to irrigate the grid with nonsense syllables.)

I I .

It hurt to be invaded by our surpluses, to wander in that crowded yet lonely Gehenna, to ask who chose these spendthrifts of architecture, these markings and commerce, the ornate cornices, spandrels, coffee machines and bottled water?

Amidst findings of anguish and lust, there was an immense betokening of intimacies threaded to the wrong objects.

The flux baffled, engarbled speech.

Yet still, a few stood proudly cut from the mechanics of illumination, their faces written upon by hopes and pains, singular and yet embossed by unplanned beginnings and ends.

They exhibited an uprightness, not of freedom, but rather as though a tree had resisted back against the brutal informing weathers of history, those mournful plenitudes, cares, bents, desires and redeemings.

The objects were now more ghostly, more unaccountable, and thus no longer those things about which banished rhapsodes were entitled to sing.

Meanwhile, the verse's flatness hinted at a tutelary linguistics, at an awareness of thought's barely inflected swiftness, of substance that left one both free and bereft.

I I I .

Philosophers proclaimed the mental light as holding this *lumina, luxe.* But grime smudged against vision, smeared the sense of beauty with the prolix essences of markers.

The light, imageless, bathed real objects, fell across her brow and face, onto contours of small breasts, dark furtive sexual hairs . . .

Less personal, the light also slatted up the city into longish beam-work, Brownian fonts of godheads, their secondary power a kind of utterance.

I V .

These dream-states implied auroras of flooding radiance, offset the textures of the brickwork, traduced them into penetrant nostalgias of barred and indexed windows, dark homiletics of streets, the coarsened kelps of entanglement.

In spite of an overriding sense of packed and sectored proximities, emotion broke from one's fears, likewise the reverse, etc., occurring as though in the trued rooms of an abiding, momentous dwelling.

Or as fantasy suggested: a child walked down leafy lanes, embracing a storybook dappling, only to turn a corner, to emerge from the glade and come upon the concrete Behemoth itself.

Therefore that other fealty to the premonition that each word was not the dawn but a nailing sun at noon?

No shadow of ambiguity on the paving stones.

V .

The calculus on the page, the numbers and symbols, the operands and constants, transparencies and theories. Only these thwart an interminable bruising against reason.

Morning's light had never been particularly confirmatory.

V I .

Sun's faint warmth as yet not fully given over to the day's shape, still enmeshed in night.

Its light arrived and with it the wheeled traffic in the street.

Time, the indulgent parent . . .

As though the mind were primitive, a forest of deep recurrence in matted leaves and balsams of pine. Memory futile, grasping at technique again.

V I I .

And what was writing? *A snail's slime down the walkway! Nothing more natural to the creature*, he wrote bitterly.

O and by the way, little soul, how is a cognizable world possible?

Is it infarct or comestible?

Only yesterday, the old Printing House Square, buildings torn down, resembled the site of a molar's extraction.

And this month, litter thickens to a matted surface catching about the feet, to ankle-turning slipperiness of compacted color supplements, the musical crackling of styrofoam cups.

But you, you are positively beautiful, done in, or, as the French say, *en déshabillé*.

Not a word for thought in this enjambed paradise of desires.

V I I I .

Evil more clear than good, wound more certain than caress—the unloved always recognizable when posed against the loved one who remains unknowable.

Face secreted in mystery, city's mystery.

What about one who lies athwart a darkness, stamped by incised verities?

Be wary of judgment, best to withhold closure on another.

Attention and skilled action, even these must suffer hesitancy.

It was the only way we could talk about streets and neighborhoods, thinking where they blend or die off or transmute to something else.

The most opaque thing is the body which you peer down at as from a crown.

Thought's pinnacle?

Easy, however, to float off with the wave of a hand, a dream of oneness—her skin and freshets of eye contact, mouth or curves, the secret places.

Thus the ruminations and the trust, estranged valuations, the city coalescing as fragile web, the familiar trickling like an open tap into homelessness.

"WE CAN ONLY WISH *VALEAT QUANTUM VALERE POTEST*."

for A.S.

The dead were to be interrogated
beside the meaning "sign."

We looked in vain for the words
"cow," "sheep," "pig," etc.

Hahriya meant not only "to comb,"
but also to touch affectionately,

to stroke, to caress, to fondle—
also to tickle and incite,

(and in the sexual sense, to be
caught in the dreams of *Puduhepa*).

On many days, we admonished
ourselves for our arrogance.

Much of the vocabulary consisted
of words hidden behind logograms,

indicative of first things,
the need and desire to speak,

to bring back the body. Thus,
who to propose a given meaning,

who to vouchsafe its reliability?
The dead did not need our wisdom.

One context would have allowed the idea
"to hurl, to shoot," another "to dismiss,

to throw, to push aside (as a child)."
The word stems were clearly uncertain.

In the documents, *eribuski*, the eagle
was made of gold, and flew over

without conjecture. But *elwatiyatis*,
with its many syllables, meaning unknown,

appeared again and again in connection
with the word for "billy-goat."

Questions remained. The void offered utterance.
We thanked the impenetrable silence for permission,

for deepest gratitude. We bowed to
the acrid muteness of another world.

Take *esarasila* (the context does not
give meaning), but we pondered its sound

on air, for we had been given the word as though
incised in stone, as glyph or diadem, as memorial.

Esharwesk translated, not only as "blutig machen,
mit Blut beschmieren," but "to become, to turn red."

Layers were many. And here, face it, we sought
another's breath, mother to our language.

We sought sound as resurrection. With this,
we were beschmieren. The gold eagle flew

toward a reddened sky, the word stem not always clear.
But better not have attempted the translation?

Halkestaru, "Watch, night-watch," was actually
two words. Difficult to have taken any of this

as causative. Still, all we wished for
was that our efforts be *harnuwassi*,

"of the birth stool," or that we would be led
to *hantiyara*, a place in the riverbed where fish live,

a "backwater." *O Valeat quantum valere potest.*
No work for the self, only lust for lost voices,

fellow *hapkari* (pairs of draft animals) . . ."

AUTOBIOGRAPHIA

Weren't you given a text? To honor the congregation, the organ dulcet,
the cantor's hum, hymnal of Europe's East, steps of sound made fugal

but laden with a weariness (joy for another day), history transmogrified
into plaint upon plaint, to be ushered into manhood, to be brought other's pain.

Early on, the *Shekhinah* gone into exile. Most of that century you saw
not love but power, cruelty, the face which laughs against the sun.

What could you do if you were not steeped in things like the others
but merely walked to buy milk or bread, heaven above, earth below,

to visit the old streets, the elm's grainy seeds lying across paving stones,
tourists milling and the Atlantic past the bridge brilliant as a sword cut.

Saline, solute, salve, this art burning to base metal. What carries one
who would sing a hymn but eddies of language—never the pure thing—

maelstroms and tidal pools, word-forms, the will hemmed in like an ocean
to its basin, rhymed to the rack of its tides. The word's ring deflected

in the baffles of the city into space, echo bounced from storefront to tower,
fading toward soundlessness—ear cupped to catch emptiness, translation

to Paradise from which speech fled. *Put down this cloth, said the rabbi.*
Cover the text and emplace the cap. Live neither in blacks nor whites.

Avert from the scroll rising above the earth, gaze upon limitless blue,
the inventive weaving of clouds. Live straight ahead. Appearance

will be your pain and mentor. Be at the threshold, not at the Ark.
And later, to go back to plucking a word from the weave,

lamé, silver, deep magenta, designs mazed over the fold, lines and margins, and underneath, as though one sensed through flesh, the delicate structure

of *beths* and *vavs* on parchment, the inner and outer of secrets.

WINTER NOTES, EAST END

to A.S., in memoriam

Finding the nothing full, I bring myself back
to the day's page, the window's revealing expanse

of snow, *bardos* tamped down upon *bardos* (*it is not
possible to contract for a stay*), brittle leaves

which sign but do not speak, the frost, the graveyard
across the road leaking its supply of portents, jargons

of elegies, white words without issue, the swan
on thin ice, images which imbue, only to lend perfume
to the acrid taste of being countried outside a soul.

*

At midnight, Orion and the Dog Star swell in blackness.
And on clouded nights, no constellation and no consolation.

Intelligence unable to code another winter night which, like
a tunnel, leads back to a helplessness only a child should feel.

*

At the window, January's sparse glories:
ice crystals adhering to rocks,

also winter birds that never quite
belong in snow-struck landscapes—

they signal what burns up old mechanisms,
the rote cyclicals of seasons, routines

into which one-way time-bound bodies are cast.
Winter making one desire—that part of it

containing stars or blankets, anything memory
clings to or words rend open. Stagnant water

reflecting back ridges of heaped up ground.
An autumnal reflux embodying a sorrow

or hunger for unfixed space. Death imagined
as a motionless mode of contemplation.

*

This world, that—I know one
should stop. Tired eyes

should rise from inked blue
lines inscribed on yellow pad.

And that the eye should elect
this hovering blur which,

if one is tired enough, becomes
spectral green as though

through writing one came
again to a parkland.

*

Do you trust phenomena? Old literalist,
Blake's guinea sun is mocking you.

These short days blend unawares into nights,
instructions in how to join the great poets.

O yon pillowed laughter! Yet somewhere,
a dog howls, and self-knowledge is suddenly

the heat of an immense banked fire. Gone now,
names sequent to things unnamed. The blank page

no mystery. Composition is, composition is . . .

*

Philosopher's stone, shrine room's hoardings.
Everything under the august calm of the sacred.

Still panic that one can't live to the smallest jot,
to the least syllable of the matter. Wasn't it called

ghost or haunting, an iota of someone left?
Remember the dead or must a kind of *iotacism*

be proposed?   Homer long ago: each beat
of the line awash in Heraclitus's river.

*

Scouring words for the relieving aura,
breathing deeply old vocabularies of sea,

of pine, ever-present tinge of salt.
Panoply of stars, planets. But often

one can't find what is being searched for,
the galaxy seemingly drained of that covenant.

Thus is it written out for syntax's rules,
for the untranslatable memory of black holes,

for voice, for love and against concept.

ESCHATON

(2009)

I

LOOKING AT SOME PETROGLYPHS
IN A DRY ARROYO NEAR A
FRIEND'S HOUSE

If the spiral meant one thing,
and the square with an incised X another

and if the footprint were deeply traced in stone,
and the spider on the rock scurried off, or if,

as Janet said, the boulders were a 'rattler motel'
but the snakes were off molting in another place,

and if our words are off not by being
in another place but in a nowhere

of no help to ourselves or anyone,
if they are just stuff and the proof of stuff,

but might as well be vanished or banished,
if they are the proverbial music of the cosmos

but no longer sing of a self, and if the footprint
is just something to aestheticize and to remember

those tribes who lived here but now go unrecorded,
if the stone's marks are the fleet music that we exist

and exist no more, if the tragic mode was a wondering
about this very fact and therefore had to go like a used car

for next year's model, stationary as an exercise bike
that seemed to drive a lot but stayed in place, if to see

the petroglyph as just *there*, exposing all this
and we are deluded for thinking elsewise

as someone, me, you, those we care for try to round
the horn of this thought because only love is at the end of it

ON A PHRASE OF MILOSZ'S

> *He is not disinherited,*
> *for he has not found a home*

He has found vertiginous life again, the words
on the way to language dangling possibility,

but also, like the sound of a riff on a riff,
it cannot be resolved. History has mucked this up.

He has no textbook, and must overcompensate,
digging into the memory bank if not for the tune

then for something vibratory on the lower end of the harmonics.
He's bound to be off by at least a half-note—here comes jargon

baby—something like a *diss* or hiss. Being is
incomplete; only the angels know how to fly homeward.

Yet, once the desperate situation is clarified, he feels
a kind of happiness.

*

Later, the words were displaced and caught fire, burning syllables
to enunciate the dead mother's name.

(*Martha* sounding then like "mother")

Wasn't it such echoes that built the city in which he lives,
the cage he paces now like Rilke's panther?

He was not disinherited.

He was not displaced

He is sentimental, hence he can say a phrase like *his heart burst*

The worst thing is to feel only irony can save

The worst thing is to feel only irony.

"DARK TALK"

At that time, the muse of our particular circle was dictating "dark talk,"
her words carrying with them the stale odor of cigarette smoke, also wine, red wine.

I'm sure of it.

For it was not very long ago, her thoughts tracked brilliant if bleak pathways,
drew others towards her. She spoke with such perfection of a world, one made bleaker

by and since her death, brought on by a mysterious nighttime seizure.

And it's we, who will die later, who now remember her talk as being "dark."
She spoke about poetry, especially. And that "scared and depressed," a friend told me

—because if one talked about poetry, talked big enough and without sentimentality,
then all its metaphors, syntax and gilded figures of speech were mere fabric

that our otherwise endless poetry talk had worn down to the thinness of a sheet of plastic,

as though one's self had been reduced to a nothingness by its own repetitions,
and finally fatigue and nonsense had made us stop.

And it was only then that one saw, glinting darkly, *the other side* that waited for her,
and waits for us, an open grave for words and ourselves

—it was only then

MY CITY

This constellation is a name
before words

no god has a hand here,

and distillates of memory

crystallize then reveal
structural flaws

unplanned as cells
gone wild in a tumor

Possibly, the bird
was once an eagle

but now a mourning dove
coos on the window ledge,

abandons its two white eggs
to the pigeon or the peregrine

The hole in the downtown
sky is of another order,

purchased from the fractals,

made one with the incalculable
past tense about to conjugate a future

ABOUT THE CAPITALS

The city and the world. The world, self-enclosed, a stone among stones,
a sculptor's marble, seamless and complete.

And the city, exorcizing itself, drains language into rubble, into erotics
and wrath. Overhead, a boreal haze is brilliant,

silence and blackness in its velvet case, by which one is disowned,
banished to an unmeant meanness

while standing on a rooftop hearing sirens and cries, those sounds
which escape to a darkness beyond us.

One would think sounds enclose, but these divide us.

And then we climb down the stairs, and our descent is edged with dull
fright.
Now no light falls, and through the curtain's crack,

as we rise to each other, the night presses toward us—an enveloping force,
as though it made this world certain.

THE HERESY

Exodus 20.25

The god commanded a naked stone be set up
and with no marks put upon it. But I had
lost that god or it had become something

like a rain one hears but does not see. I
did not hunger after others, no graven images
to make, no divinities to carpenter out of air.

I took silence into time, marking the absence
of our late vocabularies in their conspirings,
these new mythologies, as they fell from on high

through our skies and through our roofs
scouring the mind as cosmic rays leave
traceries in the cool white lime of tunnels.

DIASPORIC CONUNDRUMS

Call me not Naomi, call me Mara —Ruth 1.20

And now this man is fatherless
because he had a father,
and Israel is no more.

A line encircles
deserts beyond Jerusalem,
and he who was given a name
has lost the right to silence.

The man had a mother
because he had a mother,
and Israel never was.
Jerusalem, city's mirage,
shimmers on desert sands.

How could this be real?
Who will rise up
a name like Ruth,
put a name,
like a child, onto the air?

The dead are dead.
This is certain.
This is what was written,
why it was written.
This need not be said.

BANDELETTE DE TORAH

for Carl Rakosi

In honor of the Eternal One, it has been made,
this band and cloak, by the young and dignified girl,
Simhah, daughter of the cantor, Joseph Hay,
son of the wise and noble Isaac.
—1761, Musée d'Art et d'Histoire du Judïasme, Paris

The hunger is for the word between us,
between outside and in, between Europe
and America, between the Jew and his other,
the word and the non-word.

In the museum case, belief has been sealed
behind glass. The gold *Yod,* fist-shaped
with extended finger, marks where the letter
is made free, *davar* twining *aleph* into thing.

The hunger was once for textured cloth, brocade
of thread, gold-webbed damask, tessellate fringe,
for sewn-in weight of lead or brass, the chanter
lifting all heaviness from the page, singing out

lost richness. He followed the gold *yod* of divining,
alchemic word intoning the throne's measure in
discarded lexicons of *cubits* and *myriads.* The cloth
lay over Europe's open scroll between Athens and Jerusalem,

between library and dream. What if Athens were to be
entered only via the syllogism or Jerusalem's sky
were written over in fiery labyrinth, in severe figures,
unerring texts? The hunger was for the lost world

that lay between Jerusalem and Athens. Later, terrors
came to be its portion, flames beyond remonstrance,
synagogue and worshiper in ash. Celan in the Seine
with its syllabary. The words were as burls in woven cloth.

They lie across the lettered scroll, ink on paper
enveloped in darkness, desperate to be inmixed
with matter. The words were between us, poised
to rise into constellated night as task unto the city,

to enter *this* place unshielded between the One
and nothingness, if only to exist as from an echo
between hope and horror, between sacred sound
and profane air. Between Athens and Jerusalem and America.

THE LANGUAGE OF THE JEWS

is what carried us, though it came late,
having arrived via Deuteronomy.
All the names were given back to the earth

by the imageless God. This made the words
lush and profligate, tribal jests at best,
but incapable of speaking in tonalities of awe.

The elders exited under duress from the empyrean.
Inscriptions and maxims were as tumbled graves
in Europe pressed to the earth, pigeon droppings

on the backsides of stones—impossible to offer up prayers!
Still, love and memory flowed for the violated principle,
but where find it, beyond what horizon, behind what tree?

For centuries, it had lain between pride and *shtetl,*
then among voices choked with dirt. And once
in a while, the terrible catastrophes of a people

were written to the page so we might know
what it meant to rise to unbounded cruelty.
O distant ones, lost with the words

and gathered again only by calling forth
one's family name, from which kabbalists
make *gematria,* thinking to spell out fate.

EAST HAMPTON MEDITATIONS

I .

It is night now in the world,
and we are required to wake,
to think of urgent words,

rain, lightning, fog
lingering past dark
and beading air.

To speak, perforce,
with desire
to form remembrance,

to make our ghosts
as though sense
caught something outside,

as though, in the rain,
one heard strange,
muffled tones throughout the night.

I I .

Yes, my parents were here once,
barely unpacking their bags
before they had to leave—

dead parents,
if you are not in my words—

So all night, to feel
an urgency
awaiting the moment

when we have
shed our words
as artifact,
when we are released
out of ourselves

as offshore
lightning rends sky and sea.

I I I .

Wasn't this how the past
was to come back,
haunting in its dense compactions?

Life as pointillist,
a comic wink of a love missed,
of words unsaid,

and only the writing
had been this fog
surrounding.

I V .

Tonight,
as part of
our requirements

to make myths
of duration
from nodes of light,

while above rides
a thick
and silvery moon—

fear enters—
a risk the mists
again receive

by a conjure of
imagined voices.

V .

Why then begin to write,
but to bring back a life,
which, all confused,

is not for *now*
but to remind one
of the dead

or of those yet to come
who might utter
their necessities.

VI.

Thus to wake and sweat
for sun to burn the fog,
to let things stand plain,

to walk between,
to feel emptiness as freedom,
to remember how one lived

only in silences,
freshened astringencies,
storm-stripped,

a structure made
as though with clean planking,
new shelters of the day.

Memory, which burned
in the dark grooves
of beclouded hours,

has left you riven
with traceries,
and having lost your way
you want to honor them.

THE CHRONICLE POET

One tries pulling syllables clean, like freeing
old nails from plaster. Undoing the dismantling of
human gantries by listening, as though one had an empty
water glass to his ear, wondering about the other side,
shushing wife, child, visitor, the gnawing of a rat,
to catch sounds between these histories and our apartments.

What is overheard is mere scratching, someone perhaps
short of air, desperate, a man eating dictionaries
quickly, avidly, hopelessly. Useless, useless! Nothing
impedes thought's passage more than an unuttered word,
one desperately cut short or untimely enough to have become stuck
where it makes only a shameful noise, a beetle's endless
clicking in the throat of a corpse. A noise seeking to reach
its fundament, trying, out of pure sound, to form itself
as honest language, and by that failure, painfully embarrassing.

FOUR LONDON WINDOWS

ON KENTISH TOWN ROAD

Breakfast by the cafe's window when sound truck
blared "Jesus is Hope;" old madrigal twanged
by guitar and fiddle. Feedback from speakers

echoing off crumbling brick to spike that piety
with the present. And, while drinking coffee,
a young, still singing girl, dispatched from

the marchers, hands him a flyer block-lettered:
PEACE & HOPE. Then suddenly, to hear talk of
business in the City, of changes in the price of stocks

as they shuffle across a screen, giving out their unmeant
meanings: who to be clothed, who fed; in what wars, what
color would the people be running from fiery villages.

So much like a music which lightly touches a world,
bulked and muffled in laminates of history. And so,
the stillness when the girl has left. No word

to pierce that plane of glass, and this to carry
on his walk to the Underground, the procession
alongside him in the street. Song, music, earnestness.

He descends to the Northern line and out at Camden Town
catching again the marchers' shouted "No" to the world,
walking amid the crowds, parting that sea of resigned faces.

LONSDALE SQUARE

is perfect now, but wasn't this what the Victorians
wanted us to be, living under that perfected row
of rooftops serrate under skies, a god's knife in ascent

to jigsaw the world into its proper places. Also,
the little park is perfect—a squared-off ambuscade
that shut out the grime of mills, the young girls sold

under the railway bridge. In Lonsdale Square now,
the windows tell no truths. Fine dinner glass, they merely
hold the clouds. One looks through to neat walled yards.

SOHO

Sex-shop's open window box is curtain fringed.
I hear her say "lovely" as I go past, quick
peer down hallway tinged with pastel light.

She's young enough to make one gasp, to buy
one's self from time. The curtain strips
comb out against the air. Shot silk; no glare.

The light and forms too difficult, too obscure.
But see back to Hagar and to Sarah who stand
sphinx-like at these windows to the future.

WESTMINSTER

Silence heavy as the stones covering poets and kings.
And light, a fine wash of water and flour, spills down.
We and other tourists afloat in it, disembodied

in the pews, untethered from carpeted aisles. *Unreal city*—
its vague hum muffled in high vaulted rafters. Blake,
honored in the Corner. *Man is either Ark of God or phantom*

of the earth and of the water. Here all is prophecy and trance.
We are such baffled languages now: is a word anymore
than a window open to a space halfway between us?

Mortise and book, leaded lattice, love and body.
What is uttered, the seen movement of another's lips, brings
the mirror down, opens a transept to quickened transparency.

LIKE PROSE BLED THROUGH A CITY

Yes, I have followed them, time and again!
—Baudelaire

THIRD AVENUE

It was lovely—exeunt clouds, but I turned
      the corner, just today, to see the man
face down on the sidewalk, a model for some
      bas-relief, a thick grime impacted
into his skin and clothes, he had made it halfway
      to some kind of stone.

Possibly, in my mind, he was already assuming
      an icon's status, a little figure in a niche
which flares in the caught light on walls.
      Certainly, I wanted him exemplary, easing
the disparity that opened between us
      to remind me that the language must be clear today
and show its encumbrances, the unintended beads
      of utterance that catch meaning out of sorts,
as if to say, desperately, "beautiful days, clear days,
      exuberant days, days of light of the late
city's century."

IN ROY ROGERS

This woman takes up a lot of physical space with four
       shopping bags filled with her scores
from garbage pails. She is going by me, cutting
       a swatch out of the neutral air as though
she were mere nothing, a bit of my eye's saccade,
       my city eye moving decisively and furtively . . .

And only this iris's flicker discloses the flawed
       ratios between the physical and the mental,
as it also works in reverse, in my head with
       its minor headaches, the harassments of
finding a minor thing "too much" one day, so
       pulling back as she goes by or I go past

and then trying to analyze that guilt-prowed surge
       as though the ripple of me had pushed
the spar—once again—from her reach,
       naturally, seen from the viewpoint of the spar.

EITHER, OR, BUT

Nervous, with fear and trembling (*either*
I've drawn down Kierkegaard into this riff,
or I've not). But the sky was very blue today,
and across it only a few clouds made their way,
buttressing against the west, almost stately
as though a language of forms resided there.

That the gods should be lodged in the sky!
Forcing the eyes to rise from the street,
to look at the immense unspeakable silence.
But—and every word very much hangs on a but
these days—I was drawn by the sounds of a man
and a woman arguing while a small boy
with squinting eyes, frightened, looked
at this one and then at that—as though
one were the sky and one were the street.

I've drawn Kierkegaard into this work
because of his Abraham in terror under
the desert sky, on his way to Mirah
with Isaac in tow. Because of the child,
eyes moving, as ours, from street to sky.

CREEKS IN BERKELEY

You who cannot love a freely spoken word
find delight in these half-enclosed rills
where bittercress and wild lily mat
and so cover the sharp-edged enclosing stone
muffling the water's musical notes
as they blend or accompany the voice
heard on the street or enter barely noticed
into homes edging the small open spillways
before the water slips under cemented rock
to travel beneath streets, its force
lost at sea level where it flows from outlet
upon outlet flattening into the bay's wide expanse.

You led yourself or were you led by her who once
lived on Cragmont and whose voice has its own sweet
rill running uphill with a freedom teasing you
from any turn or enjambment until sound disappears
into the air, into a wordless breathing of light
the late sun strikes from the bridges and the windows.

II

AT WORD-BRINK

I alone, featherbedded in language.
I alone, luxuriant in speech,

How to put world there, at word-brink
among so many lovely things that flow?

Who to claim otherness in flesh,
in love-tinged landscapes? I alone.

Remembering old unbridgeable sadness.
Unable to put the case. And who,

if not I, to mourn for lost parents,
for Michael who must mourn?

In the loose talk of language,
that omnivore, so much are these

estrangements no longer
of the glib morning of novelty.

What to come of time stringing words' syntax,
inscribing us together? *I alone,*

that closed bell ringing homonym sound
of another word, isle or island.

HORN PEAK

I .

Here, I must talk now
or disappear as tattered rain cloud,
here, clutch vainly at the peak.

Bashō would have craved
the thin air,
this world letting go,
trail getting fainter,
a few blades of half-bent grass,

finally, scree fanning upward
to splayed out sky—no path
or all the path to be.

No other human,
no words identical with space.

A shard of mist
is barely a reminder,

blotting sun
until it is a false moon,
white upon something still whiter.

I I .

Late, oh it is late, I wake at night
on the mountain top
and scream out in horror
at my own aloneness.

I cry down into the hell
pure matter is.
Cannot think, cannot think.

I know I startle a few wild things
that move in the dark.

Yet nothing, not even another,
can haul me to the lip
of the life one leaves
by being here.

A DIALOGUE OF SOME IMPORTANCE

One's hand. Its whole existence.
Minuscule things it seeks to grasp.

> *the hand that moves to touch,*
> *lost by the mind before it moves,*
> *so who propels it thus?*

Her nipple. A crumb. The furled edge of a tissue.
Surely there is some charm to rolling bread
into small resilient balls, casting them off
the fingertips to squawking ducks.

> *is it only an emissary,*
> *a move of a heart in flight,*
> *to mark where, in outward scenery,*
> *it seeks to lodge itself?*

Often, I am swamped by incredible pleasure,
by the wild connection a thing makes between
my thumb and finger, as though desperately alive
in some galvanic dance. *Ouroboros* tastes his own tail,

> *self love? love's self?*
> *who guides a hand knows*
> *the horror of attached.*

but I have made deities
out of the lint of carpets,
metallic granules and snotballs,
especially out of lost eyeglass screws.

MARGINALIA IN A DESPERATE HAND

I own two left shoes,
But I also own two right shoes.

Ah, those fragmentary thoughts you failed to propose!
How they would have fit with the ones I did propose.

Yesterday was yesterday, today today,
But between the two more than a day seemed lost.

I hear that you are happy, that I am unhappy,
This fortunate news.

*

"He plays the music so loud, I can't hear my TV."
This was the melody, but where was the horn?

Fumbling for the right phrase, he finally confessed
He was 'disreligious.'

Alas, it was not a fateful hour, for the sea
Kept company with the fog, the fog with the spandrels

Of the bridge. "When I'm on my own," he shouts,
"I leave metaphors behind."

But the radio works; it's the crowd that doesn't cheer.
Furthermore, it's misspelled "negative crapability"—

Syzygy, where he had been brought by his thoughts.
Not only the planets but people aligned against him.

*

Tickets to the theater: to a comedy called Health,
A tragedy called Being, actors and audience invited

To invent the mode between. But the watchdog sleeps
On the bare stage. The marquee is dark, the strollers

Repair to nearby bars. If you squint, even
The dimmed streetlamps can be restored to prominence,

And the subway runs.

*

Where were last year's sleeping birds? "Dear Artist,
Your supporting materials can be picked up at the office now."

He clicked his tongue at this attractive, boyish muddle
Where nothing, neither doors nor windows separate

The passers-by from the merchandise. Or should we say
We can no longer endure an extended portrayal of human destiny?

Or that the ending, moreover, destroys the film?
Still, in one's dreams, one sways "like a fainting strand."

Today, the data bank over deposits white noise. The very
Voids are carefully redefined so that only jargon now stands

Between us and sweetness and light. Look for a comfortable
Niche in an otherwise impoverished medium. I own

Two left shoes, but I also own two right.

INFLAMMATION OF THE LABYRINTH

for Harvey Shapiro

As my doctor described it: expect vertigo, dizziness, spinning of the room
    when flat on the bed.

Definitely, the ear in the world or the world in the ear.

Any desire for restful surcease is bound to be thwarted.

Impingements from outside are meeting those from within.

Freud warned: the apparatus, to maintain itself must lock its doors, not
    against theft but a super-abundance of visitors.

This inflamed ear has let some extras pass by, each with a hope, each with
    a desire.

No longer is the cheese of truth to be nibbled by the few.

Usually, the hungry ghosts are left to dance on the other side of the doors
    of perception, but now they've gotten in, and like Blake, I'm twisting
    in Job's whirlwind.

Perhaps it was winter which brought this on: those winds off the snows of
    yesteryear drifting against the cochlea.

A heat pad might help or a tranquilizer, something to deaden the
    ridiculous vatic impulse and tongue-tie the mouth's motor mounts.

Yes, this passage is stopped up, the snow banked all the way to the Bridge
    and the Tower and the granite statue of the Green Knight.

Enough to fill up the red wheelbarrow or to take Rosebud for a downhill
    run in the park.

EXERCISE ON SCHIELE'S
DIE JUNGE FRAU

Sight is like water
       which to the leaf won't cling.
Yours is a young girl's thighs and ass.

I am related
       as rain-soaked to stone.
The self is what waits.

Searing shapes have been torn
       from ancient forms.
Never mind that mother suckled the past

nor that father mapped days ahead.
       The self is what waits,
and you are a hope lodged in time's interstices.

Seeing alone invents.
       Breasts high, shirt
sails from head and arms, a thrown-off banner

by which the eye's
       conqueror makes her jest.
The self is what waits.

VOCATIONAL TRAINING

There were many such compacts:
the oscillons and quarks
formed atoms that formed particles,
sand grains and jaguars,
and hats, many hats,
and tennis shoes
and sprawling cities.

And there were hearts
that corroded
on the syllable's tin,
and siren-curators of loss,
not overly bemused by order,
hawked their translations of dross.

And we wanted to talk,
we wanted to talk,
but the sounds
were surrendering themselves
to the object's private cunning.

And so we sang,
and we sang,
as banished rhapsodes
used to sing,
about the painted vase
and the molded head,
about that one possession,
our dispossession.

HOMAN'S ETCHINGS

MAPLE

Here, the paper's plane
by which one enters a mysterium
to find foregrounded
before the trunk, a branch.

And where on paper
did the burin's point touch down,
why voice over voice
and why each leaf must overlay a leaf?

Paper's edge—
growth   nothing.

ANEMONE

A sea of leaves stroked in
—different leaves—
rioting out of the same core.
Say again: sea of leaves,
trembling with the wind, *anemos*.
I speak for my own comfort. Say again.
I speak anemone *bosanemoon*,
the faint wavering,
the silk of the words.

BRETAGNE

What came first? The ruined house
shows humankind was here, the fence post
placed upright. Far off, the church's steeple.
In close, high grass one almost feels
as though walking to the crumbling brick.

Under that broken roof, the curious story:
What came first. And how it came
to entwine the wire with the rose.

TAK ESDOORN
(diptych: maple branch split by seam)

O bud, on the other side!
O parent, O child!

GEESE

Etched brambles and flat light,
and nearly too cold and brilliant
to look, to raise one's head
above the rise, the nearby stark
entanglings that form
a delicious after-sex, the drug,
that puts off winter.

                    And so,

the distant flock rises
almost imperceptible to mind,
to wheel and turn, to fade in cloud . . .
unless there is a witness,
a ceremonial: a word.

TO HOMAN: AUTUMN

You have invited me to die
by ripe entertainments, so I
make a horse's head
of fungus-crusted stump
and gaze with dead eyes
of a dog where a great
branch broke from the tree.
I count patches of lichen,
enumerate their missing tints.
Each bit of lined decay
must be imagined, eye
made surfeit with its true
entangling: dead log,
sinuous vine, thorn and bract.
Autumn. Gone is syntax.

IN THE STUDIO

for Tony Rudolf

The picture in progress was always displaying what's not there, memory's trace, as though hope were the cloud-chamber's particle remembering itself.

.

Who didn't imagine the body parts left out, the blocked perspectives, violent indifference, reveries of inattention that registered as slackness of face, all those Virgils of interior space spiraling down a psyche.

Here the god of the invisible ruled the visible, crouched like one's grim double in corners of the picture frame, truing up what lingered at the edge, wraiths of unknowing entwined in death, the dreamt worlds of longing, bafflement, desire to be immortal?

Still one sat, moved an arm at the behest of the painter.

The arm stirred.

To live, the painter's demands implied, was to commit to an awkwardness, an unstable canting forward into life, into others.

And one discovered the limb's numbness, fatigue of foot or the calf's pins and needles.

Still, the commands: *move here, sit so*, seemed right, far better than dogma or the self's ever-waiting upon the self.

Wasn't this how looking out was to become looking in, one's ghosts no longer blocking reflection?

Yes, there was to be silence, the held protest, the charged swallowing of pride.

All this in order to exist, not as in the painter's mirror, but as opacity and surrender, the continual truth that lay halfway between one's animal scent and the oily chalk's grit and smear.

POETIC GEOGRAPHY

for Rob Wilson

Lost.
>   To be lost
in that old American hope

of words
>   enfolded in the continent,
as though, while walking in the street,

to stumble
>   into a hole,
to be plummeted

to Israel
>   or China,
to fall vertiginously through space,

homing
>   like a smart bomb
from signifier to signified, and there, oddly,

identifying
>   with a lover
instead of oneself. Lost hope!

by regaining
>   that archaic love,
you are left speechless as mythical Israel

or China,
>   even as you march
onto the grand highways of nation-states,

past architectures
            of virtues and perfections.
How distant, then, that place of sublime landscapes,

of silvery tinged flesh,
            arising out of dream
or nothingness that make all words erotic
            and restores them to memorable chaos.

REPORT ON THE DISPATCHES

> *words of reason drop into the void*
> —Simone Weil

REPORT:

And then they[1] brought the receptors up.
One saw soldiers[2] who were standing, looking
frightened before the endless troughs of sand.

Grainy films of grit and oil clung to lenses
as though inert, in the dead voice of matter's
humming[3], was calling out for company with inert.

Below encodings of the tongue, the trembling halts
and stutterings had been prioritized, first in the queues
of abject sounds made incommensurable[4] and then repeated.

Such wordless brilliances—the automated incunabula
of the synapse—lay pooled in adrenal shallows below
language's hard unyieldings, blighted by fear-weeds,

which took sounds and made them narcotic. And when one
finally spoke, webbed into circuits with other warriors,
each word was presumed wedded to its proximate word

as though signalling[5] a commonality that would flash
through other shuttered apertures—say ears—
say passages normally closed off from light.

DEBRIEFING:

1. **they**—This collective "they" lived nowhere, camping out in front of the barbed wire gates of the base or on the remote fringes of the battle field, an enormous heliotrope swinging its vast head toward unimaginable stimuli, amalgams of anguish and violence. As the senior members of the profession chanted "Accuse me, I am old and I am a part, accuse me," their aloneness was assuaged, their solitude was banked. The reporter's eye no longer looked for data but sensed a focus, some prominence as the sun flared or the night flared and assumed momentary shape.

2. **soldiers**—The soldiers' lovely naïveté: sweet limbs, some marking their uniforms with odd patches and flags, offering up to the bloody-mouthed gods, their individuation, even as they approached death in the trenches. This horror.

3. **matter's humming**—Unwordable or unsayable "humming," such as that which pre-exists on magnetic tape, the bass note of the Western canon. Subject to entropy, it lacks sufficient energy to sustain itself, to prevent decay and therefore, by the most violent means, finds, ultimately, an external force (an enemy) to enable its vivification.

4. **sounds made incommensurable**—Without measure and having no meaning, hence no limit—mere utterance aimed at the other side of disaster, hence hopelessly and solely self-reflective, something like the exegesis of one's own death rattle.

5. **signaling**—Socrates, in warning against the effects of poetry, describes it as an overwriting or inscribing upon "the city within oneself." In times of war, however, there is a secondary function, a kind of ghostly telling, often too late to be heard, amounting to a sort of compromised message between a man and his corpse.

SARAJEVO AND SOMALIA

Beauty is such a magnet, the art world such a thief,
the paintings sit in the galleries of the present
sucking up the real, like mirrors for the chosen.

The poems are for the unelect, for those who discover
that words have been ransacked. Surely, the more one reads,
the more one feels a word is unable to resist paying its ransom.

This was yesterday: "I want to describe what I saw, a rib-cage
starved to bone." And something terribly linguistic about
literalness has escaped to wander among other phrases

such as: "rib-eye steak" or "chew my bone."   And these,
the broken *bona fides* of our speech, nomad memory
and pitch tents of poetry on abandoned ground.

BALKAN MOON AND SUN

for Rachel Blau DuPlessis

Language,
        it leaves us at times
in the hollow shell
        of its own tuned rhetoric.

Moon dead word dead sun word—
        we must live with what's incalculable.
Light's talc ray
        of unutterable moon as meaning's

slide over word slit
        —*stop, segue*—to fall on
her bruised body in the Serbs' rape house.
        Policy as chalk death night.

Early daylight,
        sun (dead) our witness,
the used girl murdered
        or set free to wander in male-made shame,

to make the day an atrocious *bardo*
        where moon set (dead word) coincides
in sunrise (dead) making time
        composed of light-banded contentions,

to be restructured by advisors of self-interest
        at language's back wings, and there, to find
the composed amulets of chronicles,
        the time-scored bloodied ideograms

where death

      crosses life's design amid disorder

of the piled books from which were pulled

      these ramifying words:

to love the world they stole from you:

      yellow whiteness of our common sun blocked.

THE ASSUMPTION

after a painting by Paula Rego

How else does the mother rise
        but on baby Jesus's back?

Ask his mother, he looked like an angel,
        he was an angel

Before his virgin birth,
        before Mary was even a mother.

Precariously, her head is thrown back.
        Looking up? Loss of balance?

No matter what, the boy will be burdened
        with going down to earth,

With his agony, and with his rising up.
        Already the worry lines show

In his young face. Great weights are
        first carried from and then to

A god on a wing flap. Every task
        is done at least twice.

IN IRONS

Our forebears observed rituals
of hand-held tools, of the seamed
carpentry of open boats, the beauty
of waters and of compassed charts.

And from shallows, from near-to-shore sloughs
a few wandered into open sea where the eye
shaped new referents out of wave and cloud,
to save the mind from its aloneness.

And without meaning, the salt tear corroded,
water burned on cracked skin,
the current's hold on the craft was self-
canceling in the suppressed null of the seas.

There too the tongue turned under
as though one dropped an anchor
into unformed memory, watery, adrift,
looking into the black sea for a reflection
surfacing with the force of language.

MEDITATION ON THE *BA*

—Freud kept a stone carving of the ba *on his desk*

The mind layered in word and time
       stratifies the mirror
holding the invisible presence of the *ba*

(Egypt's death bird), perched precisely
       where you are
in the silvered under-paint of reflected features.

The body, its hint of mortal weight,
       to account
for the curious weariness by which the bird

makes its appearance in the midst of a life,
       alighting as something odd, something hidden,
a disturbing blankness in our looking,

and with a blind will monstrously feasting on available light,
       a darkness which consumes. Thus:
no more mama, no papa, no favored uncle, only this *ba*

flitting behind the glass, neither a grosbeak on cabin's rail
       nor a bird of flight aloft in the city.
Only this creature found neither in memory
       nor in the guidebook nor singing at any open window.

FLORIDA

Surely you lived in the best place before you died.
Your balcony faced the bay, not open limitless sea.

Often we looked across water to the city's streets,
as before us, in the west, the buildings lightened.

And now, as if, from the fact of your dying, a child's bright
fears throw a curious light into dark gullies of grief.

A sudden knowing, opening fold upon fold of memory
that had buried one deep. This morning, who to tell

that stars had gone, that sea birds were on the rail?
For whom to wake, only to be orphaned by images?

Air upon air, with possessions packed. And look, a gull
still sits by the sill of the dead parents' window.

Who lives here? The bird caws from far outside us,
slits wide the envelope of the self. And out spills light,

intensifying fright. Things shucked off? Crates
for charities scattered about the room? To have left

the fetal curl, learned how to depart. Window cleanly wiped,
eye at horizon's edge; palms minute and sky a cloudless vacancy.

FRIEND SICK

Jokingly, his "deathward trope,"
he called it when I phoned
to let him know my thoughts
were with him in his pain.

And then came the repetitions
of who'd be there to tend him,
where he'd be and when and if to call.

Now the fifth or sixth such time
such matters had been discussed, they
were no longer mundane actualities
but ways to stretch a bind.

Thus, most often, talk turned centrifugal,
wild nodes of embroideries, a galaxy's spiraled
arms that led one out forgetful of a center.

All pleasure in minute unfoldings flung
so far a word skewed off in naïve laughter
and for a moment no longer curled
around its silent brother, sister, death.

EVENTS, SPORTING

What exhilaration: the skier leaps the crevasse
in the glacier and, out of the corner of his eye,
sees his shadow briefly flit the icy bottom.

And, yes, the pulse leaps in the self's umber
as one watches a squirrel jump to the next branch
or while reading of lottery winners and those

who come through unimaginable horrors
to make front page news. The moment gluts
with our unlived longings of identity.

But in the parent game, one calculates
like a physicist or astronaut, standing on
a ledge of the universe, signaling at another.

And from there, one has no chance to leap:
it's near, it's infinite, it's out of bounds.
The eyes of one's child are deep, fathomless.

Mere smudges at the centers of nebulae.
A pity to look there for shadows.

FINDING THE MODE

The Kabbalists found the word
shining with a God's infinite meanings,
each sound uttering a promise:
not myself, not myself, but doorways out.

Yet wasn't this what the Buddhas were hearing,
that quiet of the world in which
the contemplated bird perched on a stone
eons before its call was to be heard?
And in the background, a *mantra* droned
something like: *O not me, not nothing.*

Meanwhile, Time blundered me with its noise,
the hobble of the verbal, and I slid out
from under my Grecian Urn to walk the street
in front of the Museum. *Nice marble!*

Which is how I discovered my American
garrulousness whereby each word is air-
brushed into history like a travel poster
and so becomes a highway true to the abyss
i.e., *my eyes have seen the glory*

                              or *cross at your own risk.*

A TERROR OF TONALITY

One heard the sound—in my case, muffled piano chords—which
set up a slight saw-edged vibration as though beneath the skin,

a ripple or a wave, a curled edge lifting black beyond the mingling
at the threshold's littoral as it abandoned human matter, its matter

of being human, and then its not, and so its need to make of need
a bright consuming picture, say of a man wandering to ancient

echoing music in a strange palace or of the eye's flow over a woman's
silky texture: to make a canonical moment, a chordal microtome,

a slice of self-stopped time in time made real, an *as if* photograph,
as though a sound repeated brought a world as bind . . . great calming—

and then, the music's recession was a scouring predicate of time,
set intervals of fifth notes which caught out the minor chaos

hidden within the lucid forms, out of which echoed that *zaum*,
that wordless sound, not formless, but welling up through flesh—

forcing from the neck and its quivering funnel these hopeless
forecasts of fear, these reminiscences of thinly layered hopes,

and suddenly an identity was losing base, as if a yearning
not to be form barely shimmered through those veiled processions

of chords, and one could not, at that moment, utter words
to relieve the self's awareness of non-self, but hummed

the heard requiring no words, which went up easy, pleasurable, but
left no power in the music's meaning to meet the meaning of a life.

LE DERNIER PORTRAIT

The matter of no longer having to speak and having no one nor anything to speak to. A matter of death masks in the Musée D'Orsay. Made by one who lays the gauze over the corpse's face and pours the clay and sips coffee while it sets. When what sets is the horror of the world, of the *not-you*, and what is left is this object imprinted with your features. *Ars longa*—the day's rictus. The absurd cheating because one's last day is never even a whole day. And here's this hardened object with its painted flesh tones, the pale, lightly brushed reds, beady fakery of glass eyes. Here in a museum, though this is hardly the time to suggest there's life in the thing, even if it's keeping august company with robust Maillols and Rodins. And with money and with the grand café whose tall windows bring Paris, gorgeous Paris, close enough to touch.

Everything homes toward these frozen visages. Here's Pascal, lidded eyes, dour expression without complacency for his century. Marat and Napoleon, so popular in death, they suffered five impressions each.

And what of those who leave no artifact but this, who are only this artifact, and that by chance? *La femme inconnue*, a sort of Venus of this city. She threw herself into the river in a simple dress.

The mask shows her smiling. Did she sense that she did not belong to Paris's well-tended streets? She inhabited that other side where the unnoticed poor go, *arrondissement*s of ruin and shame.

She never belonged, though there must have been moments of half-living, of half-dying while she mermaided the Seine. She floated under the famous bridges, under their blackened barrel vaults. They were the wreaths of her cortège. She offered and was an offering to those lustrous waters, to a silence of enfolding depths, to the matter of having no one to speak for her.

III

STANZAS WITHOUT OZYMANDIAS

Who finds the pedestal finds the poem.
To know time had its ruins, its knowledge.
The traveler was fortunate.

And now sand has its texts, its mica
and feldspar, its fulgurites and beaded quartz.
The heart a display case, the eye a catchment.

Granules adhere to fire-drawn surfaces,
mineral led and glassine—acolytes of the grain
fused to a speech of unwarrantable sermons.

Wind and lightning storms roll the high dunes
into long trenches, into tides of erasures, now
smoothed to a nothingness—an abyss for the geometer

who mourned the mirror's lack, who hungered for stars
hidden in the dark behind the day's brightness.
Hard to remember what tribes wandered with Moses

or even who invoked that sere alchemy when Jesus disappeared
for the numbered days of an older Flood, or what tempted
the saints to sit in their aloneness at the ledge? Unawares,

the bush burned and the mirage shimmered. Solitude of those
who entered, who sought earthly want, though they wandered
in the skull of an angel, in the trepanned and bleached spaces,

remembering only the colorless semblances of their desires.
So now to place a word on it, like a bit of mica
winking in the sun. And now to place time on it,

as though time were the handwriting of the object's moment.
Effacement in the grammar impelling one to be only a shadow.

ESCHATON

I don't know where spirit is,
outside or in, do I see it or not?

Time turned the elegies
to wicker-work and ripped-up phonebooks.

All that worded air
unable to support so much as a feather.

*

If there's hope for a visitation,
only the ghosts of non-belonging will attend.

And now death is slipping back
into the category of surprise.

I sit up at night and pant, fear
half-rhyming prayer—

self beshrouding itself
against formlessness.

In-breath; out-breath.

Aria of the rib-cage equalling apse.

Skull, the old relic box.

ISOHEL

To be catalogued by desire,
loving even the self's falsest myth;

its rising to mind with the day,
setting in moonlight, leaving one

with a requiste sadness. Words.
Even those inevitably borrowed,

ringing in at least two heads. Words

making that song for one, while filling
another with shame or hate. All of life:

its two places. Our world is widely spaced,
and can't be witnessed as one or by one.

And this, I would say, is almost an image of charity,
a desire for another to have as much freedom as oneself.

And some will feel that to use language is a menace over *thanatos*,
a desire to be immortal, a desire to shine, to shine endlessly, wherever.

FROM THE NOTES

To find words as a kind of meeting place

even as they fly loose on unresisting air.

Not enough to make a leaf quiver

nor to alter a molecule of sand.

But then a woman's eyes are suddenly liquid,

or a saint is judged harshly by a phrase.

And what is denied is elsewhere affirmed,

if belatedly, as though one

who says the last word thinks he sets

a house to burn like straw, and one

who has said the first word must begin again.

FOR A MOMENT

For a moment,
while it is happening,
looking out on the ruins of the world,
the poem can do nothing,

and for a moment,
words fill me with that belief.

For a moment,
the poem and the ways of poetry
have the power to show me nothingness,

and make me feel, suddenly, shockingly to myself,
quite small before all those who suffer greatly,
who live in huts, who scratch to eat dirt under grass

or find themselves alive in others' ruins. Then
our politics are as a blue sky overhead—
aesthetic, useless, no more than empty speech—

languor as the poem is languor
to the political.   See: those who suffer,

who know nothing happens for them,
do not look up
as we, who can make nothing happen,

happen.

ORDINARINESS OF THE SOUL

            the dead
who gave me life
            give me this
our relative the air

When I visit
            here,
I feel as if
            I stand apart,

apart at any city block,
            but especially one
near a hospital
            where the hurt
and bedraggled mingle,

where they talk
            and bum cigarettes
and banter.
            Any city block
makes me ask:

for whom ought
            the muse to be real?
Or is her tomb
            bare, and with
an empty coffin

(as though someone
        swept up words,
bagged them for the media).
        Does it obtain—note,
I have to ask in *legalese*?

For whom
        is the world's desire
to make real its desires?
        As though underneath
an impulse

a profounder
        truth were met,
not in grief
        but from a need
 to find someone

and their wants,
        to find
one's companions.
        as they mingle.
To sense

        they too make
this same pilgrimage
        when they visit here,
standing apart.

AN INTERPELLATION

And now, they clamor
for masterpieces to burn

desperate to send up into air
the ash of Racine or the Bard,

to watch it drift down as prose
on those still listening. But I need

to talk about those works
one reads endlessly over the dead,

those slowly turned pages, half hope
and half hubris, to speak in favor of the classics

of living up to them, as though one
could rise on the wind from a worded grave

with the taste of cinders in the mouth.
No other way to make a life of ruminant memory

but by piecing out uncertainty's frightening ellipse
even as this condemns the mind for a moment

to the thoughts of others. No other way
but to be awakened to another language, to return

to a voice haunted by unknowing, to the dead's
unfilled fantasies of hope or love, to those words

capped now by finality, by a closure that cuts off
their sounds and makes an ashen sky look wider and richer.

AT WORK

These white painted offices.
These tile floors, waxed.
These fluorescent light fixtures.
The flickering as of a dulled cosmos.
And here, too, the copy machine hums
a muted hum of the afterlife, a sort of
on-off quantum of a background sound.

To look for beauty in that strange eloquent noise
as it enunciates something like the vocabulary
of the Romantics who favored life with the poetry
they wrote, a *frisson* of words pouring out
vacant parking lots of being.

Yet to be unable to expunge that ever-
ingratiating mode by which the word spoke
to its author and to its auditor,
nor could one divest the body of its mere
tinglings as the ear's tympanum became the self.

As selves around one died, selves
who spoke in their own codes, and
whose sounds in their dying floated
in the air with the hums and the light.
The ear assimilates and never forgets.

Here, late one night after an office party,
Fred, who hired me, mooned himself on the copier,
on that glass over the greenish flashing light.
And in the morning, draped the offices
with the blotted copies of his ass.

Eye level, the bleak dimples and strange
pathetic craterings were a landscape,
a yearning for some life outside of life.
It was fun but also it was a statement,
said Fred, gay, playful, but also
in the office, political. Fred died
in Puerto Rico of something they then
called 'pneumonia.' But before he went,

Fred hired, along with Priscilla
and maybe Richard, that young man, Frank,
who lasted into the mid-80s. By decade's end
though, Frank was acting strange—about him
we could talk—for the disease which struck cruelly
at his brain before it wormed down into the body,
was now something one could talk about. Frank
was dead from a disease that finally had a name.

And wasn't there another, how to say this,
on my watch, for I was doing the hiring then,
(Fred being dead and Mary having quit)
whose name I can't remember: Bob maybe?
Who got thinner and thinner but whose mind
held up until the last, I'm told, so he had
the opportunity to confront his own death
with full consciousness.

He too copied things on the machine
and walked down the hall to the mailbox,
toward the end confirming that a sick person
looked sicker under the fluorescence
that poured down on the hall between the copier
and the mailboxes where the memos go.

There are other modes, but only one mode
of the beautiful—tinged with our non-being.
Modes inflected then with death. The elegist
has no power to let things be,
to let them dictate back into the head
of one who tilts and listens, hears the lilt
of being mixing itself with the other, hears
the humming of light as a text in quest of death.

THE AGE OF THE POET

What are the book's pages
          meant for?
The world is played out,
          and mind seeks its high,

a throne above care—
          not for blessing,
though it might come to that,
          but for surcease, for stillness,

for not thinking. Dog of a poet,
          bones of words, having lost
for this age the sweetness
          of referent—Rilke the last to say

house, home, tree?
          (knowing our time demands
cold invention,
          that tepid faculty-room tea.)

No way to find oneself,
          unable to wish exile.
And always belonging
          in a wronged way.

One face, the coin of alienation,
          the other smiling as if to pay
the due bill of self-image.
          Creature of the mind-screen.

Preferences, apathy and boredom?
       Managed fate?
You inscribed yourself, then lived
       as a beggar irritated by those

whose emotions ran unchecked,
       who gave themselves
to false gods, to the idea
       of an impotence authored by others.

GLOSS

"The house was quiet and the world was calm"

History and the constellated night. We were ravished by the rungs
leading to the library, by what the poet "wanted much most to be, "

his peace, his book, his quiet—the lamp burning there upon the page—
while others in the world concocted death, the poet, believed his "wanted much,"

believed it life instead of death, and took his "wanted" to the street.

The bulk of good, desire for peace, surcease, now filling streets, emblazoned
on signs for all in righteousness to carry, such marchers were for the poet's peace,

the ultimate good, the *do no harm* of doctors, a healing or tranquility as though
harvesting the heritage of the East.   For these, the poets left their rooms, feeling

their good while elsewhere under wheeling stars, others in our world concocted death.

ECLOGUE

for Hugh Seidman

To compose by whatever light comes up

To compose as from a high place

To ride the elevator of a soul to a high floor

The city below resembling a hardened ocean, smokily awash in sun-blent air.

To see, under a thin film of smoke, plumes and small flarings

To feel an urge to be high enough

To have been taken to some upper limit from which the self is mere escarpment

A launch pad, the buoyant air a form of intelligence

Eyes following light-struck rivers that ran between worlds
    and swelled the lower bays to fat beads of mercury

To compose or, better, to recognize some part of the view will be missed

As though one looked through a peephole or gimlet

The philosopher writing of a "mind seeking, and then again wondrously deceived . . . "

To have left out the deaths occurring under bombardment, to have inscribed others

Paths followed, as though by metal fragments winging toward their homes

To recall a love or a joy as gritty as Vermeer's brickwork

In air, as though released into the sky's wide avenues, to feel that hope
   commingles with a word

In air, to sense loss as given, well, given romantically

To compose, as on a high, windy station above the harbor, above streets,
   eyes streaked by wind

At these heights, eyes aswim with a festive knowing redness.

NOW, IN MANHATTAN

1 .

Each breath is at least a half-life, a pause
Between anthrax scare and modern memory.

And each gaze lifted from the sidewalk is half-filled
With a rising moon sliced and weighted over the city.

Uranus and Capricorn not far from Heaven's triangle,
The night's space respiring indifference and geometry.

2 .

The day through which all walk is sun-diced and air-lit.
Work beckons towards simplifications: desk, task, words.

A wash of suspended particles through which paper gleams.

3 .

Rubble, flesh, sound now dispersed, mind torn by impulse
to dedicate lines to memory and grief, to one's lone solidity.

Breath, word, isotope and quantum, vulnerable to ghosting.
Backdrop as design. And phantom death shining through,

transposed across all the writing.

LETTER & DREAM OF
WALTER BENJAMIN

Messiah and geography never coincide.

After the Fall, the only bliss was silenced nature.
It reeked of the sadness of uninscribed creation.

The slow erasure of Torah's black letters,
written Law isolate amidst whiteness.

Paradises of language ought to reign,
celebrations of rising from mute space,

from infinity's ground, all the unknowable names.

*

These, as I strolled, were my contemplations.

Swans were rising from the pond in the park.

And yes, I might have longed instead for vanished reflections, for
disappearing ripples left behind.

For now, I am reduced to sending you these eighteen pages that muse on
the horrible present—on our politicians, those hastily put-up men, who
garner for themselves the laurels of the state.

They too have created infinities, blind alleys, endless monuments to
iniquities, a multitude of pains for others to bear.

They will outlive their brief immortality and leave a grubby ration of
murderous hopes.

So imagine me moving amidst clouds of dust under a mountain of books,
not to Palestine but to another of Berlin's forbidding streets.

Wiping clean the unpacked books.

They will sit on their shelves as we await fearful marching in the street,
boots stamping over their pages, coarse shouts, frenzied thought. . . .

Impossible for me to write of other topics, mathematics and language or
mathematics and Zion.

The only path, these days, my bitter words.

I do recite the litany you imparted to me.

First things: unriddle Kabbalah.

Unriddle text.

But the truth is, I found myself reading the despair I find everywhere
inscribed in this city.

Messiah and geography never coincide.

*

He climbed a labyrinth,
a labyrinth of stairs,
past other stairways
descending.

He climbed
a labyrinth of stairs,
each step tested
with his foot.

Always tentative,
always hopeful,
while nearby,
other stairs descended.

Breathlessly
he rose,
up to their heights. Chest aching,

thoughts twisting
 between his temples,
head pounding
with his blood.

He felt lightheaded,
fearing always
each step
would carry him
into the thinning air.

*

". . . and furthermore, the law's appearance should be the result of the knowledge of good and evil."

". . . all visible law is law-making violence."

"Only the law of God or of the General Strike can undo the violence of this bloody law."

I am walking, not knowing whether the heart is full.

Not knowing whether the soul is full.

I would like to keep silent.

My eye registers tree, cloud, pavement.

Messiah and geography never coincide.

THE VISIBLE

at Port Bou has been insistent, as though some god
or a god's talon were clawing at the occiput.

The sea, and its blue-green water can be seen from almost every street.

He might have looked one last time from the window of the hotel.
His grave in the cemetery on the hill faces out.

There are lures, siren calls if you like, that secure the self from rocks and
selvages.

There are lighthouses.

Others hear the lost bestrew the littoral with their voices or stand keening
in the rocky fields above the wave tips.

Enormities, they cry to their taloned gods, to swirled obscure objects
as if that same god had plowed under what can be named
or mischievously hid it in another of the sea's furrows.

*

One fears each word narrowing to a lightless and sea-depth pursuit,
in touch only with its own hardness, only with itself.

Water softens rock, that is love, and seabirds have beaks that crack shells.

Port Bou harbors its sleek white yachts.

There are lighthouses.

On this coast, stone is impermissible and sun unpersuasive.

COMMENTARY IS THE CONCEPT OF
ORDER FOR THE SPIRITUAL WORLD

If these streets, this world,   are the arena,

then each person passed,   each bidding building

unentered, leaves room   for ruminations

illumined by an edge,   a back-lit otherness

positing a liberty   to think or not think

an idea, to fly up   outrageously

or swoop earthward,   toward a grand passion

with a hawk's fierceness,   talons extended,

and yet, for a second,   to hesitate—

If we are always outside   the precincts of power,

even our own,   and so imagine

(for instance)   the possibility of a tyrant,

helpless for a moment   before sunlight's brilliance

on rolling grass,   if we no longer

keep to our assigned faith   as Job's messengers,

each escaped alone   *to tell thee,*

then the deep flaws,   the salvaging uncertainties

in the world's   overriding syntax—

love of self, for instance,   migrating to love of another—

or those records   of an observing eye

noting the lichen's patch   on the rock face,

the waters slow   eroding of the boulder,

(such witness   an ongoing work

of resistance),   wouldn't this proclaim

that *he is most apt   who brings with himself*

the maximum   of what is alien—

a sense of world-depths   that no longer crowd the mind,

thus a rich compost   of the literal

of what is said.

And then might not   our words loom

as hope against fear   for near ones,

for their gesturing   towards a future?

I V

MOURNING FIELD, NOTE CARD

Slaughtered lamb broken in the shards and rocks.

Wasn't the cycle that the ant ate the carrion,
that the bear ate the ant, that the bush
surrendered the berry without sentience,
that the merry danced and lived,
that justice was that morning
only an afterthought because
to have to think justice
in daylight, at all hours,
signaled our defeat

What broke the cycle?
He who played with the untimely
and he who transgressed,
whose bloody mouth still hungers,
who is myriads of the unappeased

And didn't we ring the cycle like a bell,
Didn't we lull in the vibrato,
drowning the world,
oh lull, oh sleep oh stopped up ears
couldn't it be said that our singing
like the tenor's with the goblet,
cracked the bell.

And didn't the lamb lie broken
at the base of the towers,
staining the dream

and were we now to forego dreaming,
to feed the black crow of the real
our hearts and our children,
to offer carrion to the pigeon,
to let our fears blot the afterimage
of the city before the siege

to remember the ancient cycle littering
the walks with leaves, the blue cool
of the autumnal skies, to walk toward
the dull sound of the bell, to hear the tinnitus
of the imaginary . . .

The mourning field has no perimeter. The mourner on his path into the depths of grief creates his own outer border, the starting block of his own sorrow, possibly the remembered moment of first awareness, the picture on the television set. Sorrow has its own space-time continuum, a yesterday or a last month when the heart was ready for its heaviness. And because the mourner is both vulnerable and political, he may cast aside the temporal frame altogether, may find that his pain begins long before his own birth, blaming history and its aftermath. For this reason, the outer perimeter of the mourning field is not fixed. It can be moved at will. It can accommodate past, present and future; it embraces anger and sadness. Since death confronts everything and confronts it uniquely in each of us, there is no telling beforehand what we may need or where to begin. Adjusting the fence lines of memory or imagination, back-shadowing our pasts, these are the operations necessary to bring us to our grief. No matter. Wherever the mourner starts, he is creating a girding for his journey, not so much to aid in mourning as to help in confronting the obstacle that stands between himself and the ability to truly grieve. A willingness to imagine death up close, to take it personally—only this brings someone into true relation with mourning.

Freud in his essay on war and death writes that we often live "psychologically beyond our means, that it would be better to give death the place in reality and in our thoughts which is its due." For a moment, for an infinity of moments, the images we saw on September 11th gave death its due with a vengeance, reconfiguring death and dying in ways Americans had only seen in movies where reality and unreality swirled together in an intoxicating mixture of vicarious danger, a danger that did no more harm than to launch celebrities and box office hits.

But now, after the events of September 11th, the images pouring out from the screen, ones to be filed alongside the others for the future, were real in a new way. No one could see these without being indelibly seared, whether one saw the buildings crumbling to the ground or the people jumping from the World Trade Center tower windows. There was even one of a couple who leapt hand in hand from a high floor, stepped together into the air above Manhattan as though going out on a date, an image deemed so awful for American television that it never aired again. Just hearing about it was enough. The television I watched showed a few such falling specks, distant and forlorn, minute against the grey-white vastness of the building. And the speck that I can't forget was tumbling in a cartwheel through space, head over heel on its way to the ground like a mad gymnast. What could it have been like for that person to contemplate the choice, to burn slowly to death or to end one's own life quickly, though how quickly would it be from such a height? Such images would tear at us forever.

On Saturday, September 15th, my wife and I took the M 15 bus down to South Ferry and walked to the northern tip of Battery Park. Smoke rose in billowing acrid clouds from the disaster site, burning the eyes and throat, and many people were wearing masks.

Slowly we made our way uptown, entering any street going west to see how close we could get to the disaster site itself. Up William Street, we peered along Fulton and Pine, gazing through the biting plumes of smoke and dust at the twisted bronze base of the north tower, the only recognizable reminder that a building had stood there. Its grid of window frames, rising to a height of five or six stories, was torqued out of shape, teased into a quarter spiral toward the sky as though by a fiery comb. Ash had collected everywhere, sitting on car roofs to the depths of three or four inches, powdering fire hydrants and shop windows and building ledges. Nothing but blacks and grays. In the disaster area, along with the lives and the buildings, light itself seems to have been reversed. Lower Manhattan was one grisly photo negative of itself.

As we walked along, I remembered that much of lower Manhattan, especially the eastern side of the peninsula projecting into New York harbor, consists of landfill, some of it comprised of rubble shipped from England after the German blitz had knocked down much of London's East End. The rock and brick had been put on ships and dumped along the East River to make space for public housing and the seaport areas. Now it was likely that all of the southern end of the island was to wear a cap of ruins, including bits and pieces of human bodies that could not be found nor extracted from the rubble. Hardy's great World War I poem "Channel Firing," which imagines the conversations of the dead war victims, came into my head. I wondered if one of us would now overhear the dead of London and of New York speaking. Or probe even deeper into the spirit-life of the broken buildings to reveal how the stones of the two cities that now had in common the destruction wreaked upon them might be communing with each other across Wall Street and Broadway on over to the FDR Drive?

In Manhattan, grief's center was, for a few days, Union Square. On the 16th of September, I walked in the park past clusters of burning candles and incense, past long scrolls of paper containing messages and poems taped to the wrought iron railings that border the walkways. Many were illustrated with simple drawings of the twin towers engulfed in flames. Copies of slogans and statements plastered tree trunks and pedestals of statues. Some had an almost political cast: "a cry of grief is not a call for war" and most ubiquitous, "an eye for an eye only means blindness." Alongside the scrolls, the faces of lost ones gazed out of photos. Grim details surrounded these: the company worked for, a floor in one of the World Trade Center towers, and saddest of all, identifying body marks, scars and moles. With words, the dead were being washed as in a funeral home, swathed in language, touched in secret places by words that only lovers or family members usually know. The disaster had traduced all intimacy. Similar photos and details papered the city. They covered phone booths and bus kiosks and were taped to the plate glass windows of storefronts and banks.

Like many faces on the notices, most of those in the park were young. They stood and milled around as young people do. And they spoke, and their writings on the long rolls of paper spoke, with that intensity only the young seem able to summon at such times as these. A few guitars were being strummed, playing old folk plaints of solidarity, weariness and misery. Overheard, the thick canopy of leaves, black against the night, absorbed these sounds, compounded and cupped them in the sickly-sweet smell of the incense and burning wax. The crowds had driven off the pigeons, but in Union Square, the notices of the dead flapping in the breeze formed a new immense flock of anguish and grief roosting together.

BECKMANN VARIATIONS AND OTHER POEMS

(2010)

the last days of drowned continents
—Max Beckmann

Beckmann Variations

SPACE

—Reise auf dem Fisch (Mann und Frau)
(Journey on the Fish [Man and Woman]), 1934

We had seen the blue spun with thin white webs
of contrails left by jets out of Heathrow,
had hoped for the promise of an infinity

that would leave a foreground for the finite,
for the savor of bodies in a room, for memory
and for this present, an entwine of emotion

and object such that its simplicity would shame
unless met head on, as one would meet an offered glass
of wine lifted in salute, the taste of bread and butter.

Not perfection, but their transitory being in the world
to be shared with others. And so we looked up to see
how wind blew the chalky lines left by the planes

into blowsy arcs, watched the waves' ruffles as they
moved down the brown expanse of the Thames,
flowing toward Whitehall and the towers of Parliament.

It was as though we were striving against a power
impacted in those buildings. And then, in the painting,
we saw the man and woman bound by silken sashes
to the backs of fish, the waves' surfaces to be breached.

And who now could live only by a word or by an image;
who could stand back, look and speak, only to fall silent?
Who, in these times, did not sense death and non-being
as a shadow, something brushed against the cranial wall?

The bound lovers in their journey are plunged downward
And must embrace fear, rapture, the throes of love, their lips
clamped shut against the pressure. Great silvery fish sound
the ocean's deeps and seed the darkness with their silence.

If you wish to get hold of the invisible, wrote Beckmann,
you must penetrate as deeply as possible into the visible.

Space is the infinite deity.

"EVERY SO OFTEN

The thunder of cannon sounds in the distance. I sit alone as I often do.

Ugh, this unending void whose foreground we constantly have to fill
with stuff of some sort in order not to notice its horrifying depth.

Whatever would we poor humans do if we did not create some such idea as nation,
love, art with which to cover the black hole a little from time to time.

This boundless forsaken eternity. This being alone,
*

"Depopulated sublime" horror vacuii
*

I don't cry. I hate tears, they are a sign of slavery. I keep my mind
on my business—on a leg or an arm, on the penetration of surface.
*

Each element was required to assume an even greater specific density
than was found in nature. This required me to leave the current path
of the Impressionists and Expressionists, it required me to make
an earlier departure on the route of modernism."

Every so often something happens to the artist that makes him depart."

ONCE THE AZTECS

—Traum von Monte Carlo (Dream of Monte Carlo), 1940-1943

Once the Aztecs learned to propitiate the gods
by sacrifice, they took no risks that the sun might
rise and offered it many hearts each morning.

Thus we understood why waiters with swords
surrounded the casino's gaming tables, and why
a young actor dressed in the robes of a King stabbed

himself in the heart for the amusement of gamblers.
The great bird of Chance, whose immense dark wings
give it range over all of life, was caged only by a flimsy

barricade of musical instruments, horns, piccolos, the
dismembered arms of other entertainers. The lost who
in desperation broke the rules or reached too far found

themselves the great bird's prey. *Deus Absconditus*
had returned to judge but found himself eclipsed
in mercy for those who made obeisance to their hopes.

THE KING

—*Der König (The King)*, 1933, 1937

He, beside the wheel, and the shrouded counselor at his back must whisper.
Niobe faces away, her bent arm lies across his sex. Eyes sunk in shade,
gaze emanating from blackened pits. Iron chair swathed in damask.
The implements are hidden under regal blankets.

The way of kings, the way of empires.
What can I still extract from the last ruins of a royal house
—how can I still make the planetary systems tremble?

Only by this—surrender. Or enable the wheel's turn.
His subjects form a chorus; they sing hymns to vibratory landscapes,
to diadems of cities. Half-lidded eye under its black indenture.
The monarch looks out from that place where his powers sleep.
Kings bear the force of statuary. Statuary seals up the force of kings.

Forms' outlines make for transitory limits. Malevolence, not an act but a radiance.

INTO THE HEART OF THE REAL

—Abtransport der Sphinxe (Removal of the Sphinxes), 1945

The Sphinxes have beautifully outlined breasts, and they stand proudly on their taloned feet. And their taloned feet rest proudly on stone pedestals. Wood for crates is stacked nearby, and a sister bird has taken flight. Each sphinx, from its platform, tells a seductive tale. Each one makes a liar out of one of the others. Whether on the pediments of stone or placed for shipment on the tumbrels, they insist on whispering silky words in one's ear. Little breezes are stirred by their sibilant words, little swirls that are worse than typhoons or tornadoes. Big storms, hurricanes are the exhalents of the world's turning, of massive pressure gradients at the poles, knocking down buildings and flooding streets. But the tiny voices of the sphinxes enter through the ears like silk worms; each weaves a gummy dream to the bones of the skull as though it were a shadow on the wall of Plato's cave. Each tiny voice blends in with the sound of the real, urgent, unappeasable. There's an official monitoring each skull who, even as he listens, is already insisting on the dream's removal. The sphinxes must be carted off. One thinks that the officials would organize deliveries of this nature in secret or at least elsewhere, but no, I have seen each one at the embarkation point eagerly straining on a rope, gleaming with sweat, pulling the crates toward the outgoing barges.

DEPARTURE

—*Abfahrt (Departure)*, 1932-1933

The master departs he always departs.
So it is with kings who sail off on boat-like thrones,
who perform the miracles of going. Don't wonders
occur when iron reason has left the scene,
and cruel profanations no longer astound us?

The king-drummer's beat is a ritual, an enclosing
rhythm of prisoners bound by rope. They look glum
in their bundles, one head up, another head down,
hair brushing the same ground on which we place our feet.

Later, there will be torture, but for now, only your servants,
these women, relieve us of slaughter. We embody the gift
of powerlessness. The king sails off, his spirit dispersed
among the males. He sails off, his spirit dispersed among us.

LOOKING WARILY

—Selbstbildnis mit Trompete (Self-Portrait with Horn), 1938

at the horn, the fullness of its bell is blocked by the doorframe as the
completeness of the man is blocked by the edge of the picture frame as the
fullness of the note that might issue from the horn is blocked as the artist
has averted his lips from the mouthpiece as his left hand has an uncertain
grasp on the horn's metal as his right hand is poised to catch the horn if
it falls as his left hand is his right hand and his right hand his left as the
doorframe is really the frame about a mirror as the eyes look at the horn with
animus as anyone can see the mirror is titled at an angle such that if it were
a real mirror and not a mirror in a painting but real on a real wall it would
not reflect back the image of the viewer.

ORDERS

—*Luftballon mit Windmühle (Air Balloon with Windmill).* 1947

The order of the profane assists the coming of
a messianic kingdom, despoiled of gods.

No act of the saint equals autumn's rotting leaves.
No autumn compares to lovers trapped in their cage

nor to the tutored souls lashed to the vanes of turning windmills.
All circle between heaven and hell.

The air transmits their stories, their cries.

But the background is as of the immemorial sea—black waves, tinged by green
globe encircling, enframing the lawful and the boundless.

FALLING MAN

—Abstürzender (Falling Man), 1950

It is great to fall, it will be important if I plunge
this way, as it would not be great to be entangled.

But if I plunge head down, feet clear and don't catch
on a building ledge, I will swoop past the structure

blazing in flames on my right, go past the open window
to my left where one sees some compact of love, violent

and contorted, is acted out. I admit, it is great to fall, great
not to fear snagging on the buildings to the right or to the left,

wonderful to fall free from clouds swirled in turbulence,
passing toward the blue of the sea where a small boat sails,

where gulls fly like avenging angels, and the momentous inevitable
wheel of life and death has a benign dusty shine. I am going down,

dropping toward the cannibal plants, the cacti and venus fly-traps,
unnameable greens and jaundiced yellows. Down.

TRIPTYCH

—*Argonauten (The Argonauts)*, 1949-50

THE WALL IT WILL HANG ON

He was born Diomedes, but a centaur renamed him,
so then he was Jason to Pelias, the king who feared him
because, as Pelias's dreams warned, beware the one who
wears only one sandal, and this is how Jason came to court.

And Pelias, rather than kill the young Jason on the spot
(the boy's relatives were in attendance), said to him "Go
to Colchis for the ram's fleece." Pelias knew those masses
of gold curls were guarded by a monster who never sleeps.

Pelias was also haunted by Phrixus's ghost. Poor Phrixus
rode the wild ram to escape being made human sacrifice
by Orchomenes. Poor, dishonored Phrixus. When he died,
his corpse lay unburied, its ghost yearning for its body.

To lift the curse this deed cast, Pelias needed corpse and fleece.
And if by chance, Jason succeeded . . . well, it would go well
for Pelais either way. So Jason built the *Argo*. His crew,
those heroes who would later spawn a thousand myths.

Also he took on board women. Among them, rage-carrying Medea
and at least one invisible, interfering goddess who whispered
into Jason's ear words about fate, honor and the glories of the future.

RIGHT PANEL

All we are sure of is the chorus.
No single voice can sing as loud.
Frail ones empowered—thin staves
bundled with others to gain in strength.

Now unafraid, the small-minded
utter warnings and imprecations
or make a chorus of strident music,
notes stitches honor to mass identity.
Lute, pan pipe, hidden drum, voices
erasing doubt. The songs will make
the heroes do anything, will foretell
how it ends, will say hope lies in the journey.

LEFT PANEL

The woman (Medea?), poised with sword,
sits on the death mask of a head she has lopped off.

The bearded artist paints her as he would a violent king.

CENTER PANEL

An old man climbs the ladder from the sea.
Jason, beautiful boy, and Orpheus, lute at rest
upon the Argo's deck, are gazing at each other.

The bird of wisdom and prey perches on Jason's wrist.
The artist's eye as if painted on the bird's head stares out
 to signify attentiveness. Jason, under an eclipsed sun

around which revolve two planets. Jason, admired
and in love. Always, the artist's eye swerves toward
nourishment. The artist's eye is looking out at us.

FRAME FOR THE FUTURE

A chorus of lovely maidens sings to quiet the waves
to harmonize with the gods that bless such voyages.

Medea has slain artifice, must slay her children.
Jason, self-absorbed, sends off the bird

who will seek ship's passage through the rocks.
Song continues. Two panels to make us compare.

Three to arouse uncertainty. *Argo*: hull, mast, spar.
The canvas is its sail . . .

DEAD-NESS

—*Tot*, 1937, 1938

As if days were not for sanity, we encountered a blinding centerless light, a radiant light, as from a diademed god, hungry for sacrifice, feeding on human restlessness.

Who can write out cruelty as an antidote to cruelty?   Who will prophesize or conjure dream-states that resist event when only the dead sense any ceremony to the horrific world that surrounds them?

The coiled serpent, time unto eternity, makes ready to strike. The monkey-angel, trumpet and penis erect, mocks from the ceiling over the coffined body whose last breath enunciated a history that gave terror and dread their public edge.

Have you found the secret mental limb of art, the appendage that like a phantom arm or leg outlined in thick, black strokes, drags us uselessly as we move through the world?

Who will write the elegy to human powerlessness in an archaic tongue?

Between self and death, we are torn by obligations and desires to which we owe the moral duty of our fears.

Other Poems

MOTHER ASLEEP

after a painting by Leon Kossoff

What if the mother
        is always sick,
what if for her whole life,
        she is sick

—when we were children—
        weren't we
always asking: is that sleep
        she is sleeping

or is it a slide toward death?
        What is it
to be always in fear,
        isn't that ridiculous,

that one's hug
        or one's moving too near
could hurt?
        Isn't that *hurtful?*

Don't these thoughts
        pend on a life
like a painter's heavy impasto?
        Don't they distort

what he paints,
        bending it from one
understandable realm
        into the fearful next?

Seeing her in the chair,
           her head atilt,
or lying on her bed,
           the child's eye

inevitably trailed
           away from her being there,
followed the lines
           formed by the drapery of sheets

or by the downward flow
           of hidden limbs,
—gravity pulled at the eye
           and fated it.

And isn't this why
           Kossoff painted
a bright red blotch
           just below his mother's left hand

—nothing structural
           in its being there
—nothing in the image
           or design to fix it,

—red blot
           of a child's anger—
formless,
           homeless—

didn't it wander
           like a loose speck,
like an errant cyst
           in a teary eye?

NOTES: R. B. KITAJ AT MARLBOROUGH

Do for Jews what Morandi did for jars. . . .
Second Diasporist Manifesto, by RBK

'small' pictures, dull brown canvas,
rills of paint—bravura strokes

petering out

luminosity had been his fame
—now subdued, brushed lines muted,

ghosted as were his Jewish ghosts
his beloved Scholem, a wrinkled tilted egg.

Arendt's face pressed against a green
vertical, one eye blocked

Jerusalem!

what, for him, did her acuity miss: Heidegger
or *Shoah*'s horrors, vast beyond banality?

he's Kafka's Gregor on his back with questions,
Sandra *Shekhinah* gone, *gone*, but still, in loving

paint the daubs float on thick fiber
"leaving," "gone," the words punctuate

his second manifesto, death as a "Jewish Question?"
impossibility of a breakthrough, of an answer

to—

WITHIN THE OPEN LANDSCAPES

words for the etchings of Jane Joseph

1 .

Doesn't the picture say
no room in this world for anything more?
If you desire to add something,
you must begin again
and make your own world,
including what has been missing
from the very beginning
of the world.

You must make an enormous effort
to leave this world for that one,
something like dying, if not quite.

Each world is so complete,
terror and emptiness
accompany every effort to leave it.

2 .

Black parts of things
keep the eye centered on the dark.
At least one can see
a bit of upstanding twig
leads to the branch,
leads along the branch
until the branch
foregrounded before flowing water
invites a sojourn past woods and house
along its banks.

Clouds are always on the move,
and suggest the weather's alterations.
Darks do no more than keep the eye
centered on the dark.

3 .

When the things of the world
are so carefully depicted
—when we see such things—
surely we surrender a little, giving
ourselves over to the thing seen.

I have heard others speaking
of the tree's *treeness*
or an object's *being*.
I have looked,
and each time I experience something
—my own disappearance,
my own failed going-out
to meet the tree,
to meet the object.

Nothing coming back.

4 .

I can love a picture
but only if it doesn't love me.
I insist on boundaries.
I can hate a picture
without it hating me.
I don't insist on boundaries.

5 .

The branch of the sycamore
forks two ways,
one limb sort of down
and flat across the paper,
the other making an upthrust
so powerful it begins
to curve back on itself
as though the light was the light
of a nourishing self-regard
and the wide-spaced faint scribble
marks that go near the vertical
were the accidental pleas of space itself
warning against hubris.

6 .

So many bridges, foot, railway, auto,
each obscured by the surrounding designs,
are mythologies of difficult contact.
Or child's stories where ogres
are secreted in dark patches under pathways
by which we connect.

7 .

The daffodil hangs its heavy blossomed head.
Wordsworth has shamed you.
And Eliot made the hyacinth
the flower of rebirth
into death's blossoming

You are lone upon the heath.
You are between realms,
between cliché and astonishment.

8 .

And let the picture transform you.
Let this thistle put on its fiery fall color,
and let its bunched tufts
resemble a wrathful deity,
and let the corolla be a necklace
of enlaced skulls, and let homage be paid
by the ground underfoot,
its otherness crushing
ego's unreasonable hectorings,
and let the mind never rest
in the false nirvana of vegetative happiness,
and let the bumble alight,
thick-dusted with the pollen of awareness.

CAPRICCIO WITH OBELISK

Bowes Museum, Barnard Castle

We followed the pictures
and the pictures followed us

the way religion follows a soul
and tries to contain it.

Did the one who suffered
come into a place

where a thing belonged neither
to Caesar nor the Sanhedrin?

Not the physical object itself
but what it gave off

or what it meant to us,
and why therefore

someone owned it.

Was there, in that martyred life,
some surcease, some pause?

And earlier, did Socrates
admire the hemlock-filled cup?

Why did we stand
before the firestorm in Tiepolo,

seeing it burst over worked-in horses,
chariots and reins   clouds scattered—

no, shattered—by light from the sun?
How did others' immense suffering

tutor us—those blinding rays
that streamed as background

to the picture's paraphernalia,
illuminating our blessings?

Was it knowledge of an illusion?
Those who made art

in the death camps, only to die
—what did they leave us?

So much were we given:
the obelisk in the faux garden,

an amusement, a painter's
whim of juxtaposition?

We were being given artifice
and asked to embrace it.

Thus, the life-sized swan-clock
in the glass case carried

implications of destiny,
but was also a joke,

its hammered plates "afloat"
on watery ribbons of silvered metal

A key was turned, sound
came out as from an organ

and the space was "filled
with Mechanism beating Time

with its beak to musical chimes . . . "
The whole shimmered

and all clapped hands at the ingenuity.

And nearby, Goya's *Interior of a Prison*
lay somber and flat,

a series of increasingly diminished arches,
light darkening as the eye followed curves

back to where Time had stopped beating,
to where Time was not.

And so the images followed us
with their baggage and hope.

The graven became sacred,
became as a shelter

—the man on the cross
and the Jew in the pit—

these were given as ours to contain us
in paradise and in dungeons.

NEW POEMS

READY FOR SUNSET

Mars is not at perihelion.

Mars is not near you.

Mars is arrayed on a skyline
as though waiting for dark.

Mars is up there, neither accepting
nor barring.

For all we know, Mars has its visor shut.

Mars—so many for Mars, all we could ask for.

Mars, Mars, somewhere floating over mountaintops.

Soon we will see Mars. We will see its light,
blood-tinged all the way to Sheol.

ANTHRAX IN OCTOBER

10/10/2001

Public air the enemy,

and the city
a million hope-filled
bathyspheres,

each with at least
one face
masked in bubble plastic,

and with a grin
a silly grin at being alive.

When thought veers like a cab
going past an infected building,

say farewell to politics
and philosophy;

invite the new language,
hysterical with its dread.

All the psyche wants
is its yellow submarine

while bacilli calcify lungs,
the brave lose their meaning:

no use military deployments;
gone, the old reliable fire gods.

Nothing for an army to do
but retire generals to rest homes.

At the abandoned table,
the roach will crawl omnipotent

over funeral goods—
not a thing for epic or ode.

Who can remember emotion
recollected in tranquility,

elegy muffled in cloth
over mouth, word's breath

just another carrier of the germ.

MAAZEL CONDUCTS "ARIRANG," IN PYONGYANG (26 FEBRUARY 2008)

> *if you leave me, your feet will be caught in the mountain passes*
> —from *Arirang*

If you remain separated from me, your dreams will be blocked as though by snow in mountain passes.

If we are apart, our dreams will shred on mountain crags, while beneath them, the passes lie open.

If the snow in passes has melted, freshets of water will run down both sides of the mountain.

If the flow of the brook begins because of a thaw, we can say winter lasted just enough, and we need no more.

If the wind makes music in the icy branches of trees, what sort of music does it make if hard wood clacks against wood?

If after all this cold, the wind is heard amidst bunched leaves, will it be the music of the past, the future or for just now while I hold my hand in yours?

If we hear the same note, will it be like walking in the light of the one moon though we are in different places?

If the moon shines between clouds, won't the icy paths gleam as we imagined in the story books, unearthly but bidding?

If we take the paths up through the passes, will we come upon figures descending toward us, some with arms outstretched?

If your feet are cold, come, at least warm them in the hut that sits astride the ridgeline that divides our two places.

LOGOBIOGRAPHY

Letter will lead to letter.

This you knew when first
you spelled a word.

Later to learn that a word
can be a kind of madness

leading only to another.

Isn't this what you knew
when words first made a poem?

(Unreasonable, vulnerable—
until another word,

like a visitation,
scythed through.)

*

This you knew.

Hearing a poem,
you knew this.

Those days—casting words about
until a line promised

to echo nothing
that you'd heard

And then, this you felt:

to make such a life
had been required of you

when first you heard a word.

SENTENCES

You want so much to know
when knowing is nothing,

when you are the one
I least know.

You want a name.

You want a word,
and with that,

the word returning
to cancel nothing

I know.

TWO-TONE LANDSCAPE

Stopped once. It was a little strip
of building by the road, Midwest.

Midwest, mid-sex. In the middle
of America, antipodes. Poplars

flanked the street. Yes, the street
had tree-lined flanks. Dry poplars.

And in-between, a view, sky blue.
An American here backs down,

backs back, stumbling into a sweet
pea-sized infinite. Withers

to the height of a grass blade,
to seed asleep in form. Roots

will grow and conform and reach
the alum-tainted water and those doors

with their polished sashes. Air, dust,
lust to phantom a low orange moon

hanging in the sky, another rock.

CITY: MATRIX: BIRD: COLLAGE

for BettyAnn Mocek

Sense of birds still in the city
of the endless city, inviting and destroying

grasp of the bird's talons, truth's grasp
rigid and hard against the swirl

that drags birds and all, our shoring,
our *we* amidst the battered who are avid to live

who know only of the bird in the city
as symbol, as focus for our lostness

and for the city walls we confront that are to us
as air currents propelling the bird off course

high up, flight-bound but struck and blunted
against headwinds, torque of circumstance

my own shaky heart, birdlike, bird, salt pulse
of a song of a bird crushed in a cage, bird at the park,

thousands of birds screaming down the sun
their tremendous noise as though they took up

our polyphony, dodecaphony of voices who despair
and sing bird cries, song, music of the caged birds

embedded, beating with the rhythm of a bird's wing,
uplifted, and then turned from their pathways

—as they are not—meeting air or not quite vanquished,
their shining Brancusi hardness, and some have become

seabirds wheeling, not so much cruelty but what is actual
in eye and beak and possibly a bird marking fresh tracks

to the moon's loft, to the bird aquiver, to the fear-bird's
white wings, and what birds have flown off I will find

in glossaries—where they exult in the cry of nothing
—in being ghost birds, cages, a hexagram of bird lime,

of time or blackbirds, a dozen birds of the myriad birds
come and go, bird-lime on the building face, but one bird

listens to a bird on a tree serenade a fountain, bird book
the message? birds fly overhead, going north birds

gather above cities how the birds come back: mind birds,
returning birds, winter birds, Egypt's death bird, great bird

of Chance, invented birds, Memory bird, like a bird *I live*

SANGRES DROUGHT

after Oppen

ground hard,

not a metaphor

seed sits on top of clay

germination

beyond ambition

beyond lives

only in interstices

do worlds' words

spin beyond the inertial

the complicit

the cowardly strengths

of the complicit

what has been hoarded

inert heap

on the seamless ground

when to speak of rain

the rivulet

the furrow

DEER AND VOICES ON THE HIGHWAY

—Royal Gorge, Colorado

"I wanted out a lot."

"—wanted to live like last night's
half-moon shadow of trees on grass
or as if I were daylight's wildflower."

"Couldn't understand
how I'd fallen in against this,
bought that other junk."

"Every night that summer, TV blared,
I'd get up, go out on the deck, *my god*,
there's *The Dipper*, has nothing to do with me."

"The black valley and cows lowing, car lights
on Greenhorn's ridge like jewelry or webs,
        wonders we weave to live,
yet not that one is small and must kneel
and suppress rage before the great mountain."

Followed the others, the road
winding through pinyon
and juniper, pulled over
with the rest, the trucks, RVs,
three deer right on the road.

Nothing unusual
to exit or come back to,
let the deer's tongue
lap salt from my palm,
a lover's touch.

LOOSE ODE: COLORADO

STROPHE

I've been here before. Last week, at poolside in Boulder, a man lay on his back reading about spiritual themes in the poems of Wang Wei. But that's what's done in Boulder. A young woman dove into the pool, breaking its placid surface only to rise from that surface again exclaiming: "I'm angry; I'm enlightened; I'm . . ." (she dived under again). Boulder. Where Air Force jets wing south to the Academy and the tile edge of the pool is bright red, the lip of Maya's basket in which world, sky, trees, woman, contrails ripple invitingly. That was Boulder.

ANTISTROPHE

And we visited the Great Stupa in the foothills where a gilded Buddha sat. Thoughts of Tu Fu walking amid temples and pavilions, remembering he "used to write of such things, wielding my writing brush." And that evening before the morning when the towers in Manhattan fell, from our motel window in the Springs, the lights of NORAD on Cheyenne Mountain flickered. What was antenna? What was starry night? The missiles ticked in the mountain's depths. The monitors' green tracks descried the movements of small nocturnal animals.

EPODE

Who speaks in Horace: "good to lie under some ancient oak, or deep in the tall grass"? Or "Rome wrecked by her own strength"? Who writes, "and now, I'm alone in the Sangrés. Blue and distant are the surrounding peaks"? Here the jets wing north to the Academy or NORAD or Fort Carson. I'm dreaming away the afternoon reading about the *kudung*, the relic body of the cremated teacher—bone and ash, being and non-being intermixed, the words leaving this world untouched but for a faint shimmer. Hot today, and I'm nodding over my book. If I were to doze off I might dream myself a bird or the eye of a pilot banking over Boulder.

AFTER BAUDELAIRE'S *LE GOUFFRE*

He knew the syllogism
        could not explain
why one day
        slammed into the next,

or why it hurt
        as much to be alive
as knowing something
        bad awaits you.

Why awls of doubt
        painfully nicked
a groove in thought,
        why hopes deceived.

The syllogism
        could not explain
those green islands of desire
        that lie deep inside.

No lines of verse
        in the logic's rationale
to carry him off, nothing there
        to puff out ego's billowed sail.

The syllogism paid no attention
        to all the half-heard talk,
to the nonsense of spun-out thought
        that only entertained.

Thus was the abyss
        carried within,
setting my hair on end,
        while winds of fear passed frequently.

It hurt as much
        to be alive
as knowing something bad
        awaits you.

He gave over night
        to Morpheus,
to seductive figures that startled
        and made sleep suspect.

Dream and nightmare insisted:
        death really
wasn't good enough for us.
        He wasn't sure:

were we mortal or immortal?
        That's why it hurt
so much to be alive,
        knowing something bad
awaits you.

FOR CARL

A Chinese poet walking, about as fast as you walk, strode among cloudy peaks looking for the Temple of Accumulated Fragrance. Somewhere, he took an odd turn and found himself in Golden Gate Park in San Francisco. Before him was a pond. He gazed down at a goldfish, swimming lazily, its scales gleaming in the sun and wondered, "if I meditate, I'm afraid I'll I find that that Temple of Accumulated Fragrance which I have been searching for all my life is really in Secaucus, New Jersey, no?" Immediately, he pulled himself up straight, breaking the trance, and looked ahead, only to find he was facing a bit of Americana, a monk who resembled Allen Ginsberg *davening* and reciting in a Yiddish accent, "Vee are lo-o-n-ely, lo-o-n-elier than Villiam Car-los Villiams before a mirror." "Oh boy," he exclaimed, inner mysterioso, "the company is interesting, but is wisdom always this crazy? The only fragrance I want now is of paprika, the hot kind stirred into my goulash. I know just the diner to get it at." As he started to move off, his gaze lowered to the pond, and at that moment, the goldfish leapt into the air and fell back into the water right on top of its own reflection, dispersing the image among the ripples. "Ah so!" or "A-Okay!" (depending on the translation) said the poet to himself. "I am enlightened, I was enlightened," and he is, he always was.

RIGHT AFTER THE TITLE PAGE

The copyright page of my new book from the UK states, "the right of Michael Heller to be identified as the author of this work has been asserted by him." I'm afraid those words are not exactly true. Not only did I not assert anything, neither the name "Michael Heller" nor the words "right" and "identified," but other words such as "work" or "author" scare me. And that phrase "to be" is quite problematic. Such language leaves me a bit sick. In fact, I've had to raise my eyes from the page to remember that the room, the ceiling, the sky, are the only arenas of longing. And that meanwhile, I'm still looking where to go, what hallway to wander down, still haven't entered into real concourse with a word since I was a babe and shouted *mama, mama!* I know, a name certainly makes one think he exists, but, sorry, I'm not going to look in the mirror to see who I am. Such appearances are not worth *bupkis*, my mother used to insist when I grabbed some toy and said "mine" or "Mike's." I didn't write those words above, didn't even proof them on a page. Perhaps I was meant to declaim them to a crowd, wherever a crowd might gather. You want to hear them again? Here they are: "The right of Michael Heller to be identified as the author of this work has been asserted by him in accordance with Section 77 of the Copyright, Designs and Patents Act 1988." *Whew!* Isn't that a mouthful. OK, now I've said it, but don't you believe it. I don't.

FIRST AVENUE

The question is always nearness. Is it
in history or in the code of constellated night?

Is it to be approached by the soul's seven
invisible rungs that lead to the library, or do I go

by the route of the young bearded Hasid who,
on the street, tears in his eyes, presses into my hand
a printed note: GET READY FOR MOSIACH.

His rabbi is dying on the 11th floor. Sun shining,
I squint as I look up. There's abundant light.
I'm getting there by looking at abundant light.

FOR NORMAN

What does the word proclaim?
If you decorate it with a tassel
or with a *tallis*

and put a picture by,
a graven image,
and add the sacrifice's flesh
and add the altar on which
its throat is cut

and add in circumstance
and add up circumcision

what stacks up time in the diaspora
free from paradise, unfree from paradise
like a creature unsheltered in the open
a creature like yourself

the word is wedded, the word proclaims
itself as bridal canopy
above your head

A F I K O M E N S

for Harvey Shapiro

NEW YORK CITY

Later, when we gave up talking about ruins,
about the demons who made them
and the contributory demons in ourselves,
I felt a need to note how much I missed
what I had barely made an effort to see.

How one day, some months after the event,
and with no heed to what might be there
in the eye's corner, I crossed Sixth Avenue,
head turned downtown. I was looking south
to where the towers had been. And suddenly,
all that unblocked sky was a reminder to me.
                          Images
flooded back as though I were looking through
a kind of window between buildings, a window
between souls, an opening that might lead me
to the Jewish god, or at least to that place
where one could imagine His presence,
where one might even place the prohibited idol
or graven image, something to bump up against,
to bow down to, to fill the space.

BEYOND ZERO

According to Rosenzweig,
God has removed himself
to the point of nothingness.
And according to me, mankind,
has been removing itself as well,
unsure of its mode, unsure of its path—
back to the trilobite or fated to remake the planet
in the image of a grand, blinding supernova.

But I do know the one I love in the singular
has taken on an existence beyond the point
of any *somethingness*, more like the taste
before an aftertaste. I'm at least one step removed
from that removed God. How to explain it?
When I move my arm out to hold her hand
or to touch her on the shoulder,
she has already moved with me.

HYPONATREMIA

The nurse said, there's no end of depth to plain water, meaning that water
was, chemically, *bottomless*, that there were no salts to cling to, to exchange
—and so, with each sip, one slipped deeper into its pure blue-white abyss,
until a seizure occurred, and the body shook for a few moments as though
in a wild propitiatory dance that signaled surrender or the invoking of the
void. It was the body then, the body curled up like a fetus guarding the very
last of its sodium, its potassium, those elements, as marked in the periodic
table, those bonds that chain us to the universe.

HUNGARY

The monuments to the warriors rise
above the profiles of the Buda hills.
They punch a hole in the sky, whether
seen from Pest or from the Bridge of Chains.
At night, a spotlight shines on a glittering
bronze sword or a helmet carved of stone.
The light punches a hole in the darkness
over Hungary. In the National Museum,
the next to last room is devoted
to the Holocaust and the Nazis.
A dull lamp illuminates the dusty exhibits,
as though a diaphanous, obscuring cloth
were thrown over its glass cases
with their atrocious artifacts, matte black
as the night of time itself, sucking up
the otherwise bright light of a national history.

MON COEUR MIS À NU

I was born in Brooklyn, lived on Pulaski
between DeKalb and Throop.
Odd place to learn about Baudelaire's
three great types: warrior, poet and saint.
But my father was in the National Guard
and in 1943 marched up our block in khakis,
a thin black holster belt across his chest.
He was packing a .45. And at night, playing cards
with his buddies, he'd call up the corner deli
for a dozen pastrami sandwiches, sours and the works,
moaning into the phone *how sick he was, how all alone he was—*
his friends tittering in the background—could someone *please*
deliver the food to the house? To my mother, he was a savior,
a saint, throwing away a fortune to help her through her heart trouble,

to keep her safe. And to my grandfather, Rabbi Zalman Heller,
his son was a dime-a-dozen bum, an apostate, running away to sea
when he was only fifteen. Later, he made movies in South Florida.
The production company went bust fast, as did his real estate agency.
He wrote poetry.

SHARING

There's nothing like sharing Jewish history in Paris.
The plaques of the dead are everywhere,
and the plaques about the hundreds of *élèves*
taken to the camps are affixed to the wall
of every school where history is shared.

Each part of the story, false or true,
pulls on one, as one tears off a nubbin
from a baguette, each bite hurts
and affects the whole, each morsel
is dry enough to make one choke
as though choking on the whole.

There's nothing like sharing Jewish history in New York.
It's like snapping apart a square of matzoh
or taking a hammer to a pane of glass. Where
one has shared history in New York, there are
only shards and splinters, bits of matzoh *farfel*
to mark the spot. Always the pavement lies
underfoot, always, while the heel grinds
the rest to dust, one has in one's hand
the piece entire.

NATIONAL GEOGRAPHIC

The poems in so many books
are like the barnacles I've seen
in photos of whales, studding
its head and carcass like an old man's
warts and liver spots. There'll
come a time when after I've read
another poem, taken another sounding
of the word's depths, all that reading
will weigh me down, mess up
the relation of my flesh to its ballast.
I won't be able to rise very far
from someone else's deeps.
The sun in the blue sky will shine
like a little disc of poetry
way up there above the surface.

HISTORY

Among the "dirty Jews" of the past, none were as dirty
as those from Poland's *shtetls* whom the Nazis
and the next-door neighbors fell upon with unprecedented fury.
It was no different for the snobbish German Jews
and for the unlucky Sephardim who carried,
like kindling, their utter misplacement, their proud
badge of dignity, into the century's fires.

AT MY FATHER'S GRAVE

This pebble I put on your gravestone
is not to weigh you down
but to bring you up. This pebble
found at the curbside of the cemetery road,
the road that leads to the office where a record
of your interment is kept. This pebble
will mark that your body has gone back
to mingle with earth and with rock,
gone back to what is inert. This little stone,
which can only be itself. I part with this pebble,
as you have parted with what you were
in this world of stones and of bodies.
This pebble is a weight upon a stone,
a weight upon a weight, a presence
upon an absence. I do not part
with my love for you. It is never apart.

TIBET: A SEQUENCE

After Segalen

AUTHOR'S NOTE

These poems are loosely based on the writings of Victor Segalen, whose work has spoken deeply to me for years. In his short life (1878-1919), Segalen, a medical doctor for the French navy, traveled extensively in Polynesia and the Far East. Like Gauguin, with whom he is often linked, Segalen was one of the great travelers of indwelling, of otherness. In his little-known "Essay on Exoticism," he explores "the notion of difference, the perception of Diversity, the knowledge that something is other than one's self. . . . Exoticism's power is nothing other than the ability to conceive otherwise." In his Odes suivies de Thibet, *he takes up his interests in Buddhist and Taoist thought, attempting at times to mimic the language of the Sages whose genius, compassion and knowledge of the illusory self he venerated. My own poems are written in the spirit of Segalen's phrase "to conceive otherwise;" which I believe to be the poet's essential task. In following Segalen's habits of mimicry, my work involves an opportunistic, even perhaps exploitive mingling of Segalen's thought and language with my own. Playing with his words and with mine, I have called these poems "transpositions" and not "translations." All along, my aim has been to conjure through language an imagined, timeless "Tibet," a place not only of great and rugged beauty but of spiritual instruction and ethical hope.*

This profound air, voice gravelled with age, wind of kingdoms

rising over the stale odor of the past, over departed moments,

filled now with unimpeded echoes, distant, brined with memory

of the sea's ages, yet barbarous and hoarse as an assailing reflux.

You are gritted with its powder of sand and brick.

But you do not arrive from malevolent plains.

You do not mark your descent by those geographic plateaus

nor from elsewhere—lost days rimmed on the abyss of time.

You do not carry that burdened water, nor have you quenched

the people of the wastelands: you take yourself unslackened, ignorant

of polar tundras, of savannahs, of gilded meridians that surmount

the intangible absence of weathers, characterless over any landscape.

Imagine! still, you are rich and sultry with non-being, intact and fresh,

as though time were again descending, suffused with old wisdoms.

And despite my self-disgust and my lethargy,

you come, a handful of air, to resuscitate with the vastness of your caress.

TCHONG KINGDOM ELEGY

> *... in the mode of the "elegies of Tsou"—unending,*
> *gloomy and distressed songs of spiritual seeking,*
> *their groans of exile and monotony result*
> *in repeated sobs by the poet*
> —Victor Segalen

I am the one who encompasses this kingdom
      of the discomfitted.
I leave behind my grasping self, and that rank concupscient aroma,
      departing, prunes my ego lightly.

I go forth to present my two palms
      lifted; my palms, knowledge!
And to those others that condescend with their pacifying balms,
      I welcome them as well.

But that same one who hunts me,
      bring him, doubled into myself, to be with me.
It is he that I search for in this place,
      my new king.

Master and servant in the same friendly body,
      see, I disperse and I unite.
Order and revolt are this place's sparring dictates,
      in common with my enemies.

Doubt

Familiar spirit! If nevertheless this is what you wish to be,

a high sovereign, sky lord of the lit temple,

one who has spoken, embracing the bowl reversed in air,

the majesty of blue, of jade and of iron,

truly, if you are a construct of that which you proclaim:

being, light of all and everything, and one who rises up to and yet

remains fixed under the roof of the great void, surrounded like a wall

of spiraling ether, profoundly hard and pure—

still what deprivation! What prostration of the orb's height

where my forehead reigns at the resting place of the sages,

over the trebled paving that rounds out their image.

What humility belittling my face.

What nakedness raises me toward yours?

What unreasonableness growls as though infused with lightning

from the lowest places where, sifting among the self's particles,

I am the mere pivot of the millstone that grinds.

Resolution

Is it necessarily thus, beingless one, that you could be

not undeceived?   Not yourself, the cancelling dust collector.

Not the disappearing.   Not transparent. No aim?

Not always, confoundingly, the lone one of your self-vows?

Without doubt and without end, evoking your certitude,

feigning knowledge, I strike three times at my own demons.

I laugh at respect. I glare feverishly toward those at bay.

I strongly sound out hope and distress.

Without fear, heart exposed, flooded by light and water,

I raise with two hands my appeal. I reach out to touch.

Manifestly, it is necessary that you appear to me:

Your sky is not futilely distant, nor your clarity.

See: I await you: I keep the dance to myself,

carrying my spirit, calling for you in the world,

throwing my weight in reverse so that I probe—

a diver plunging toward vertiginous depths under the ice cap.

Contemplation

You are, *all at once*, all that you are.

Your true essence and your numerous assumptions,

your names, your attributes: a world your world overwhelms.

Contemplation transformed into rapture.

You are the lord of science, a body more light than smoke,

thus penetrant, burnished until you are pure spirit and its echoes.

You are rich in years, first one, born from chaos.

You know how to discern the imbecile from the hero.

Glacial, Comforter, Divined Diviner.

One. Exorbitant. Contemplated. Contemplator.

In all that is animate, in which all returns and dies.

Heard. Numerous. Perfume, music and color.

Double. Dome and God. Temple formed of the vault.

Triple. Hundredfold place of the ten thousand ways.

Worried father of all who are bewitched,

your perfect eye profoundly hard and beautiful.

Arousal

So beautiful, so perfect in opposition to the human

that I am silenced—my words nulled,

never attaining to the ninth sphere

nor to the space below nor to the spirit lords who have fled.

Most high, let us walk the ordered esplanade!

Let us carry high the numerous and the just whirlwinds.

Let us grasp the circle: let us catch the assailing blue.

So high? Without hope: there are no rays.

To aid here: the new embers of our appearance.

Here the three mountains and the renewing of the hours.

Recommencing: strong interior life.

So we must let them blaze! Let us devour flesh and blood.

It is necessary to arouse one's self, its fire crackling, to burn red.

To penetrate one's heart with the deepest of gouges.

To traverse on the vertical fires that the sky stirs,

carrying ourselves to the level of the horizon filled with winds.

Ecstasy

Am I really here? Am I, an upstart, so high?

Great peace and name and splendor before and after,

touching the chaos where the sky no longer hopes,

closing itself and flickering like a round eyelid.

Like a drowned one flowing toward the other surface,

my brow newborn in fashion on the horizons

I penetrate and see. I take part with reasons.

I hold the empyrean, and I have the sky for mansions.

I enjoy to the brim, all my spirits. I provoke

my widened awareness to all the senses so quickly

that the spirit is like air. I overflow without limits.

I spread my two arms. I reach almost all the way.

Mediation

Here the self's ransom and the crude mediation;

here falls the torrents of rain and of gratitudes,

the sky spilling tears on the fullness of me.

All abundance, a cataract pummeling me.

Dizziness weighs down the flesh and the earth's blood.

Futility of flight so high without lure:

vulture frozen in the blue: agony without death.

To cut the links? Not even a giant dares.

And then all disposes itself and then all is closed and gloomy.

The yellow taken back. I am to kneel down. To flatten.

On my face, the master's eyes, the eyes living but without brilliance,

the spirit exhausted, the heart too breathless to beat.

Truly, he has been what was—

Sovereign, lord of sky and temple clear

who has spoken—the bowl reversed in air.

This of your majesty, of blue, of jade and of iron.

PATH

Of the wings . . . No. The plumed flight has only made it to the summits
    of the peaks

        where games of hurricanes do not carry.

No longer the slight shining shiver that tames itself here in this rhythm.

        This transit jolts the rock under the footprint.

To the right of life to the will of death, scornful of the sea's plain,

        of a hard base I approach your hill,

Bod o To-bod, O Thibet! place of the harmonious world,

        I dare for you this exalted poem.

Not an actor but a bird who nourishes itself on rice or grain.

        Vain turning of the pin of verse (line)

or the redressed effort of the million times of breath,

        new beak in the ice of winters.

And leave the man to himself to sing the verb from his own mouth.

        Drowned under the floods of languor,

can I chant to my own body in your grandeur,

        this driven hymn, this sky-given

tribute to the climbing rise to your highest country! .

        My heart, which beats itself with every word.

HYMNAL

At this time, when song does not follow closely the common measure,

       abandon those useless word-games that survey existence.

The new rhythm leaps and bursts the old measure:

       path to the highest of starry skies

where the celebrant celebrates. Word-haunter of old liturgical places,

       prophet wickedly enraged by the figured horizon,

reciter of discipline, conduit to the bacchic spirits,

       never itself winded in its climbing,

containing itself well—its madness sweating ink into the abode,

       fear caught in an immense self-spectre.

Unopposed by the mountain's heft: Horeb or Sicily's thunderer,

       petit Olympus or sacred Dokerla.

Thus, on their ridged rumps, a rhythmic rise and fall of peaks and crenellations

       yawning over rejected valleys,

where from lashings of words, cadences of avalanches—

       those troupes of blank sequences—

the world's magic will make up its roof.

       The hymn never so profound as when it hangs over you.

EMPERORS

As if I died a diver in the brackish sea, foul to the taste,

      or was a choking swimmer of dust amidst those calm flatlands of nothingness,

or tasted death lukewarmly, as it hesitated, immobile, gentle over my bed,

      still, I would not censure breath,

its ardency—a cry within its own calling—its memory a bronzed voice

      of the first sovereign spirit.

A lost Tibet, bonded to my apparition—this changed world—virgin, enormous,

      thrown beyond the mountains of my desire,

shouldering sky-ocean of a strange headland.

      Foreign king, whom I face and make of myself this gigantic prostration,

before space itself hardens.   Uncertain feet, swirling earth and waters.   Here

      all tumbles from on high—

water and space and feet and yet, I do not know what brings terror

      as I descend toward these majestic creatures—

self-same humans, robed, bull-like and horned with passion, possessed of grasping hands.

      Sovereign, intrude and interdict henceforth

these giants, lacquered red and grand, with saintly-seeming faces that step into delirium,

      that slake thirst from skull-cups, lively, inebriate, yet discontented.

Borrowed beingness, non-human Tibet. For its forehead imagine an ice mask.

(I see only these strange animal faces . . .)

Imagine the yak's muzzle, its long, lugubrious face; imagine the knotted limber of horses.

(I see only these strange faces . . .)

Your blazon, shorn of realms, of the mind's complexions—pride guarded by *mahakalas*.

(I see only these strange faces . . .)

Tibet, I wish to say to you: sudden vision of true being, birthed into another clan entirely.

(Humans who have severed their mystic mirages!)

Sweet sadnesses underlying all of our depraved remorse.

I wish to say here: these countries of the head are alive.

Two eyebrows on the foreheads of playful lovers, eyes heavy, a breaking thunderstorm

—as though peering into deep mineshafts in which gazing is fearful.

These self-godheads! I wish, Tibet, to tell you of these.

O semi-moving, semi-breaking of the voice and its phantomed after-taste.

All of being to the horizons is encompassed. In the net of speech, in the true world's

speech, there is radiance that never loses its integrity.

Earth! Earth! Super revelation of the continent more than itself,

    a king crowning himself by his own power,

so that through him his vassalages that come and go are self-actuating diadems

    carrying the ransom of their knowledge.

Those who hurl themselves, their feet thrust in sandals, clawing at demons.

    They who tread across the earth as though free;

following long serpentine waters, born of straight forward jets from these mountains.

    Grand rivers searching for equilibrium

through gorges and unnerving projections, rolling, flaunting, slobbering.

    They conduct themselves to the embouchures,

to the final basins dissolving in deceptive sprays, finally running

    to the sea, dropsical, blurred.

The sea mountainless, the sea decapitated as though cured of its leaden grey ennui.

    And we who dance like she-bears before its waves, we . . .

Wonder! From here to there—to those feet, climbing—hailed.

    The sea, alien in its self-possession!

It carries itself enroute, in its own studied slavery,

    towards you, vehement in your solidity.

YAK BLESSING

On the continuum, entering with first breath, as though espying beasts in a caravan,

I explore the white times, the undefined space, cutting

through stage and resting place of this incarnate adventure.

By the most overwhelming deductibles, self's trace offered

as abandoned jets [*throw-aways*] to the infinite hours.

I remember lessons, instances of ecstasy without remorse.

I have seen, for instance, herds of great yaks, eyes dead as rocks drained of rain water.

Looming sinister masses frozen in the grasp of otherness,

my vision hallucinated in their spell.

I have seen great yaks soaked with rain—having been required

to traverse the outer precincts, they are now taken to the monk's door to be blessed.

Heads with beautiful large horns,

dry muzzles full of life and emptied of death . . .

But more appallingly dismal,

I have contemplated their eyes, trembling with a crude suspicion.

The monk freezing, an irascible lump of holiness

forsaken by husband, wife, child, isolate before an impossible agony

—I have seen the man angular and rigid in his block of ice.

OF THE LIMITS

for Nathaniel Tarn

To me, Tibet, my *aide-memoire*, to me, here unexpectedly, an obstacle.

    Here, the frontier of the finite—we know the finite cannot

be surpassed, but we are called to transfigure what we know.

    Therefore, I must live, Tibet, despite the debacle, despite the invaders.

Let my pleasures and pains be adornments of time, of a nowness

    that gathers all we know.

Here, let them be hoarded to confront the great river of infinitude

    that co-exists with the finite.   Give what divinity is possible:

        let us explore.

I feel with my foot this cliff face, this self-owned fault,

    this bridge of a self arcing between illusions of heaven and hell.

Is the rock wall of my being a solid or the warp and woof of an atmosphere?

    Is the weave made of iron chains? Is the self grown thick on itself

or simply, profoundly swollen by others?

    What will ferry me over the torrents at Ta-Kiang?

Its waves send out invented beats into a vast mysterious flux.

    The teachers called this river Brahmaputra, cascade of shimmering light

flowing out of the Himalayas, a shock to the senses—as amazing as the flight of the enchained being's arrow of hope,

a vertiginous missile, spending itself from rock to rock.

If I do not let myself go—if I dwell in the self's abyss, wishing for time,

wishing for time's pulsations—this river winding in its great length,

finite and infinite, will be nothing but my shroud.

THE FORM

in memory of Armand Schwerner

Has a man sculpted this effort, has a minor god-being sketched these bodies,

innumerable and shapeless, expressionless, cryptic, self-secret?

Are they all cut, polished, restored to their stature? Do they radiate

an overflowing confidence, do they embody the fullness of themselves?

The good potters of Being who do the turning, turn their happy gods like clay pots.

Are they children when it comes to mankind, their muddy hands errant?

Does the base earth flow without laughter; is the form ultimately a masque to be quenched

in tears and under the eye of some spiritual henchman repeating the
same mistaken form?

Flippant artisans who dare no more than to recreate the *bon vivant*, the cosmopolitan

—their workings, Tibet, are not like yours.

For you, Tibet, your kneadings are raised to the great self-contained strength of yourself:

you create the molded hero, struck down and touching,

no mere potter but a poet, no maker of art but of poems.

Tibet, not from outside but from within.

Severe statutory deity, emergent chisel and fire and glowing rock,

you strike your planetary medallion.

Your great proper work, devising your scaled motto:

"Mountains, sculpture of the earth."

So these villagers have risen into their petty joys, into their besotted adventuring—

dividing space as they march forth into the day,

heads high, inserted flippantly into the furrows of the clouds.

They move as one determined mass, dragging me along, toward the sacred mountain, Omi.

They wear beautiful clothes bedecked with the flowers of dead azaleas.

What a grand party as they go.

They are decorated like beasts, perfumed with attar of mystery and transgressed boundaries.

I see their glib preoccupations; they are smooth talkers, nimble and lighthearted.

Men, garbed in red, women in turquoise. Lithesome, they carry themselves like captured lords,

their torsos curved, graceful; their faces courteous, but of a sovereign vagabondage.

O young women, each arrayed like an armored falconress, arrested in flight.

exhausted yet ever hoping for release.

O young men, gazelles of the blue harness! It is necessary to see the spirit

neither in rut nor in similar mystical embrace, neither flirt nor imploring streetwalker.

Enough to be like one who has received a glancing blow to the shoulder of his spirit.

Enough to climb towards truth from this grandiose sensual, flexibility.

Suddenly, in the blur of grey fog, in confusion and shame, terrifying and sordid

I invoke your immense ornamentation, bright unearthed metals

and stones gathered from the mountainsides, fashioned into armor.

The endlessly circling garuda, bird of time and death,

breastplate of silver, cap adorned with jewels, mantle well-made.

Tibet is an encased goddess. Foolishly, I judge you harshly, o teacher,

mocking you like some merchant from Ladak, then drooling over your goodness.

But, at heart, I am more miserable than you. So, in shame, I grasp
your being,

your mountains, precious stones, lakes and rocks. I, who hope never to fail
henceforth,

who have barely the power to think of you, to pronounce your name,
"Tibet!"

Help me, my own ears are still stoppered, my ear hearing only the inner gossip
of a grasping self.

So far, the consequence of precious words seem small and base.

Tibet, do not efface me nor leave me too humiliated.

My name comes back to me as in a glance from the book of ciphers.

NOTES TO THE POEMS

The poems in this collection are presented in rough chronological order. Volume titles are in capital letters, poem titles in bold upper and lower case italics.

A LOOK AT THE DOOR WITH THE HINGES OFF
(A chapbook published by Dos Madres Press, 2006).

Poems from the 1960s, many written in the Spanish seaside village of Nerja from September 1965 to October 1966. This collection is dedicated to two close friends and early influences, the late Ernie Raia (1937–2006) and the poet Hugh Seidman (b.1941) who were both students of Louis Zukofsky at Brooklyn Polytechnic. I have been talking about poetry with Hugh Seidman for over forty years. Ernie, like myself, was a technical writer and worked and commuted with me to Sperry Gyroscope in the early 1960s. "A Note on the Poems" from the chapbook, reproduced below, adds further information as to the context and influences concerning these poems.

> *All the poems included here were written nearly forty years ago. In my late twenties, I came to poetry via a bizarre, accidental and blundering path that began with meeting former students of Louis Zukofsky who worked, as I did, at Sperry Gyroscope in Garden City, Long Island. They, like me, had technical backgrounds but also interests, imparted to them by Zukofsky, for poetry, for the making of it. We all lived in Manhattan, and traveling together to and from work, we talked of almost nothing else but poetry, the poetry scene, magazines and books. At night, we met again in bars or at readings where the conversations continued. I began to write. My one and only poetry workshop was with Kenneth Koch at the New School where in 1964, I received one of their poetry prizes. Shortly after, I left for a year and half in Spain and Europe. It was in the little sleepy fishing village of Nerja on the Andalucian coast that many of these poems were written and published. Hannah Weiner, close friend and one of Kenneth's students, visited in Nerja and took away a sheaf of poems. Six months later two of them, "Air" and "Fragment," both collected here, appeared—my first publication—in the Paris Review. Shortly after, they were anthologized. I try to re-imagine what went into these poems, the experimental climate of those days, love of Weburn's 'pointillist' music, the background, not yet fully formed, in my love of poets like Williams, Creeley, Oppen, Olson, Zukofsky. Heady days, lighter days—looking back we can always find signs of where we've been. But I also find in these poems, portents of an open, hopeful futurity.*

Ok Everybody, Let's Do The Mondrian Stomp

Piet Mondriaan, Dutch painter (1872-1944), changed his last name to Mondrian after 1912. The poem is based on Mondrian's *Composition in Red, Blue, and Yellow* (1937-1942) in the collection of the Museum of Modern Art, New York City.

Lulu

After she died, I dedicated this poem to the memory of Hannah Weiner (1928-1997), longtime friend, who I met in Kenneth Koch's New School poetry writing course in 1964. All names are fictious except for LOUIS CAPET, (Louis XVI, King of France, guillotined 21 January 1793).

5th Harmonic

The title refers to one of the standing wave patterns developed by a plucked string. The 1st harmonic (or fundamental frequency) is the lowest or most base-like in sound. The 5th is higher pitched, possibly closer to the human voice, and, according to *newagedictionary.com*, "expressive of lovers as well as creativity, hobbies, children and business investments, whatever you want growing and developing."

E A R T H   A N D   C A V E
(Dos Madres Press, 2006).

A mixed-genre work of poetry and prose, written in 1966 in Nerja and completed in New York City during the first months' return from Spain. Only the poetry is reprinted here. The "Introduction" in the volume, contains more information on its creation and contents, and is reproduced below:

> Nerja. That first night, my wife and I descending from the bus at the depot, already late June, 1965. The air, warm and ripe, acrid with the freshly laid manure wafting off the surrounding fields. Could I breathe this smell, could I breathe at all, given the powerful disjunctures I sensed I was creating for myself in the year ahead? Pepito the hunchback, sent by the landlady, to carry our bags to the house we were renting. After four months of continuous travel, we suddenly found ourselves nearly weeping over this sudden domesticity as we crossed the threshold.
>
> Nerja in the 1960s was a place in transition, and so was I. Franco was then in his seventies, his hold on power waning. The full repressive structure of the government was still in place, but there was talk of political change, of what was to come after. There were already harbingers such as the open political talk and occasional small demonstration for civil rights in the streets. For a couple of years now, Federico Garcia Lorca's brother Paco had been returning to Nerja in the summer months. Spain's second great poet, Jorge Guillen arrived with his son Claudio and his wife. Even the local grocer, his voice dripping with sarcasm, referred to the Old Man in Madrid as "my Jefé."

Much of the writing here was done "on the ground" so to speak, at my desk on the second floor of our rented house in Nerja's Calle de la Cruz. Some came shortly after my return to New York City. For me, the journey to Nerja had been an unarticulated commitment to writing, to poetry. I had given up job, apartment, seeing good friends, to reorient my life. These pages then are a quick register, haiku-like and notational, of the dissonances, not only in the transformations I sensed going on around me, but also of the twists and turns within me as would-be poet, semi-tourist and sentimental traveler. The strange, beautiful caves of Nerja were both constant metaphor and reality for the process I was undergoing; to the extent that I was a spelunker of its passages, I was also a wanderer of my own inner life.

White plumed reeds
"yerba buena" refers to the particular local species of mint, which varies from region to region in Spain.

Kops's
Bernard Kops (born 1926), British playwright and poet, lived with his family in Nerja for a few months in 1965.

ACCIDENTAL CENTER
(Sumac Press, 1972).
First full-length collection, incorporating one poem, "4:21 PM on St. George's Clock: Film," from *Two Poems* (Perishable Press, 1970).

Pressure
"NOVI" refers to the *Novi Vinadolski*, a Yugolinia freighter that, in the 1960s, plied the Atlantic from Brooklyn's Erie Basin to Morocco and the Mediterranean.

The Cardiac Poem
"Blaiberg's heart": Philip Blaiberg (1909-1969) was the second person to receive a heart transplant from Dr. Christian Barnard (South African cardiac surgeon, 1922-2001, see section 4: "Barnard, white coat and stethescope"). Blaiberg survived 594 days after the operation.

The Body, A Fable
"The clumsiness Nietzsche/cried against": This poem draws heavily on Nietzsche's "Zarathustra's Prologue" in *Thus Spake Zarathustra* (*The Philosophy of Nietzsche*, Trans. Thomas Common. The Modern Library, Random House, 1954).

Taurus Poem
"we are at the beginning of a radical depopulation of the earth": from "Route" by George Oppen. *New Collected Poems* (2008) p. 201.

Operation Cicero
One of the best known espionage stories of World War II, is "Operation Cicero," concerning a spy working for the Germans in the British embassy in neutral Ankara during World War II. A film of these events, based on the book *Operation Cicero* by L.C. Moyzisch was made by 20th Century Fox in 1951. It was entitled *5 Fingers* and starred James Mason as "Cicero," the spy, and was directed by Joseph L. Mankiewicz. See also the life of Cicero (106-43 BC), Roman orator and statesman who, in the time of the dictatorships of Caesar and Anthony, championed a return to republican government.

Maro Spring
Maro, a small fishing village in Spain seven kilometers from Nerja.

Downtown After the Galleries
I met the musicologist Verna Gillis and her husband, the sculptor Bradford Graves (1939-1998) in 1966 on the *Klek*, a Yugolina freighter sailing from Tangier, taking me home to New York City. A photgraph of Brad's sculpture is on the cover of my book, *Wordflow*, a drawing of his adorns the cover of *Eschaton*, and other drawings throughout that book introduce new poetry sections. Arshile Gorky, Armenian-born American painter (1904?-1948). "Gorky's eye." refers to an Arshile Gorky's painting. "All things I haven't got are God to me" are Gorky's words.

4:21 P.M. on Saint George's Clock: Film
St. George's Episcopal Chruch is on Stuyvesant Park in Manhattan. The "little hole in the eye" comes from George Oppen's poem, "Five Poems About Poetry." In the poem, Oppen attributes the phrase to William Carlos Williams. "beyond the limits of all subject matter": Robert Delaunay (1885 – 1941), French artist, exponent of Orphism, an art movement that made use of abstraction and a kind of proto-cubism. "*upon one double string*" from "The Extasie" by John Donne.

Telescope Suite
"Palomar" (Mount Palomar in California) and "Wilson" (Mount Wilson), major astronomical observatories, house two of the largest optical telescopes in the world.

The Process
Dedicated to Michael Martone, the photographic artist, who did the jacket photo for *Accidental Center*.

Birds at the Alcazaba
The Alcazaba, a Moorish fortification in Málaga, near Nerja in southern Spain. Built around the middle of the 11th century to serve as a palace for the governors of the city. See also in *KNOWLEDGE*, "Málaga: The Palace Garden."

KNOWLEDGE
(SUN, 1979)

Acabonac
Acabonac Bay and its harbor are on the Peconic Bay side of the South Fork of Long Island.

Bialystok Stanzas
Bialystok in Poland, where the Heller family comes from. Great-grandfather, David Heller and grandfather, Zalman Heller, were both rabbis in the city. After the anti-semitic pogroms of the early 20th century, the Hellers emigrated to New York, along with a large number of "Bialystokers" who formed many institutions in their new city. Much of Bialystok's history, including the community in New York and the destruction of its Jewish population by the Nazis in World War II. is contained in David Sohn's volume, *Bialystok: Photo Album of a Reknowned City and Its Jews the World Over* (1951). Sohn's book is the basis for much of this sequence. *Living Root: A Memoir* (SUNY Press, 2000) cantains more information on Bialystok and the Heller family. In the section "Senile Jew," "*dy-yanu*" (also spelled "dayenu") comes from the Passover seder song and means: "it would have sufficed."

After Montale
Eugenio Montale (1896 – 1981), Italian poet, Nobel Prize Laureate, 1975. See also the poem "On The Beach."

Málaga: The Palace Garden
See note to "Birds at the Alcazaba" in *Accidental Center*.

Poem of America Written on the Five Hundredth Anniversary of Michelangelo's Birth
"the senator on the podium": Senator Ted Kennedy of Massachusetts.

At Albert's Landing
Albert's Landing is a public beach and park between Springs and Amagansett on the East End of Long Island. "*The naked very thing*": from "Childe Roland To The Dark Tower Came" by Robert Browning.

Objurgations
To "obgjurgate": is to strongly reprove. "Nagy's Photograph" in section 3, refers to a picture by László Moholy-Nagy (1895 – 1946). The title, given in the poem, is "*The Structure of the World*." The reading mentioned in section 8 was given by the American poet, Gary Snyder (b. 1930). "Tu Fu" (712 – 770), Chinese poet of the Late T'ang.

Speculum Mortis
The title translates as "death's mirror." In the Middle Ages, death was referred to as "the doctor of grief." See Philip Aries's *The Hour of our Death* (1951)

Interminglings
"Westcliffe," in Colorado, a small mountain town under the Sangre de Cristo range.

On The Beach
For Montale, see note above to "After Montale." *"a la Fellini"*: Federico Fellini (1920 – 1993), Italian film maker, famous for the exaggerated grotesqueries in his films.

Stanzas on Mt. Elbert
Mt. Elbert, the highest mountain peak (14, 835 feet) in Colorado. *"Wanderer in the Clouds"* is the title of a painting by the German painter, Casper David Friedrich.

Figures Of Speaking
The "older poet" in section 3 is Carl Rakosi (1903 – 2001), one of the original "Objectivist" poets.

Near Guernsey
Guernsey, Wyoming. A cliff face on the outskirts of the town is inscribed with the names and comments made by travelers who followed the wagon trails heading west.

IN THE BUILDED PLACE
(Coffee House Press, 1989).

With A Telescope In The Sangre De Cristos
The Sangre de Cristo mountain range runs south from Southern Colorado into New Mexico.

Father Parmenides
Parmenides of Elea, fifth century BC philosopher, whose metaphysical and paradoxical writings greatly influenced later philosophical thinkers, hence the "Father" often attached to his name.

Moon Study
"O bright!/O bright!" are from the Japanese poet Myōe (1172 – 1232), often called "the poet of the moon." The haiku is famous for having been written with only one character "bright."

Coral Stanzas
Osip Mandelstam (1891 – 1938) Russian poet who, in his poem "The Admiralty," describes the building in these terms: "a frigate or acropolis/gleams far away, brother of water and sky" (trans. Clarence Brown and W. S. Merwin in *Osip Mandelstam: Selected Poems*, p.5).

At Beaches Again
Guglielmo Marconi (1874 – 1937), one of the earlier inventors of wireless radio transmission and creator of Marconi's Law in radio physics, set up a transatlantic wireless station on the beaches of Newfoundland.

In The Builded Place
The epigraph is from Blake's poem "London," also the line "marks of weakness, marks of woe." "Consciousness in concentric whorls" is taken from the writings of Pierre Teilhard de Chardin.

Asthma
"The shock-waved halfway house of hope de-domesticates to splinters": the image is taken from a Civil Defense film that depicts the effects of a nuclear bomb blast on human-built structures.

Photograph Of A Man Holding His Penis
The poem is based on an image by Michael Martone, artist and photographer, (b. 1941, and not to be confused with the fiction writer of the same name).

For Paul Blackburn
Paul Blackburn (1926 – 1971), American poet and translator.

Sestina: Off Season
"A realibus ad realiora," Latin for "from reality to the most real," from St. Augustine

Outside A Classroom In Nerja
Nerja is a small tourist spot and fishing village on the south coast of Andalucian Spain. See notes for *Earth And Cave* above. "*Ayer, cinco pescadores morir*": headline in the local newspaper, roughly translates as "yesterday, five fisherman died"

Tourist's Cave
Outside of Nerja is its world-famous caverns. A thorough geological and archeological description is given in *The Cave of Nerja* (Patronato de la Cueva de Nerja, 1971). For more impressions see my *Earth and Cave* (Dos Madres Press, 2006). "Larios's estate" is in Maro, the next town east of Nerja. The Larios family, manufacturers of Larios Gin, was in the 1960s one of the wealthiest in Spain.

On A Line From Baudelaire
"The dead, the poor dead, have their bad hours" is a translation by Robert Lowell of a line of Baudelaire's: "Les morts, les pauvres morts, ont de grandes douleurs" in "*La servante au grand coeur dont vous étiez jalouse.*"

Climb To An Ancient Chateau In France
"Lastours": a hilltop "bastide" or fortified place near Carcassonne, scene of one of the last battles led by Simon de Monfort's papal forces against the Cathars during the Albigensian Crusades (1209 – 1229).

Fifty-Three Rue Notre-Dame De Nazareth
The epigraph is from Louis Zukofsky's "A". "*la malbolgia lumière*": a coinage invoking Dante's rings of Hell with Paris, the City of Light   "Impossible not to be gripped,

etc. . . ." is from Baudelaire's *Modernité*. "Again I lean on the rough granite. . . ." is a phrase from Czeslaw Milosz's poetry.

Some Anthropology
The idea for this poem comes from a letter in *The New York Times* of January 8, 1988 signed by a group of anthropologists under the title, "The Gentle Tasaday Are Merely A Persistent Hoax," which was a response to an earlier article in the *Times* of May 13, 1986 entitled "The Tasaday Revisited: A Hoax or Social Change At Work?"

In A Dark Time, On His Grandfather
"The just man and the righteous way/wither in the ground"—Zalman Heller was said to have written a Talmudic study in German entitled *The Just Man and the Righteous Way*. See *Living Root: A Memoir* for more on Zalman Heller.

For Uncle Nat
"The necessary ten": to open the ark and begin services in a synagogue, ten males over the age of thirteen, the *minyan*, as it is called, must be present. The poem was written to celebrate Nathan Heller's 80th birthday.

Accidental Meeting With An Israeli Poet
The Israeli poet is the late Yehuda Amichai (1922 – 2000) who taught at NYU in the 1980s.

Palestine
"Baudelaire/watched the Negress in the street stomp her feet/and imagine date palms."—this image is taken from Baudelaire's poem "Le Cygne."

Mamaloshon
Yiddish for mother's tongue or 'native' language.

A Night For Chinese Poets
Much of this poem is indebted to the poetry of Li Shang-Yin (812? – 858), the T'ang Dynasty poet, noted for his anguished love poems. The strange flavor of his work can be glimpsed in one of his most well-known lines: "one inch of love is an inch of ashes," taken from the translation by A. C. Graham in his *Poems of the Late T'ang* (Penguin Classics, 1973). The "Untitled Poems," translated by Graham, show a poet suffused with a painful and longing voyeurism, trying to see his lover, the "glow behind the screen; wish to go, cannot." The phrases: "which once forced the elements" and "brooding on the uselessness of letters" are from Tu Fu. See also below, the note to "This Many-Colored Brush Which Once Forced The Elements."

This Many-Colored Brush Which Once Forced The Elements
The title is from a line of Tu Fu's in A. C. Graham's translation of "Autumn Meditation" in *Poems of the Late T'ang*, p. 55. Almost all of the lines in the poem contain the titles

of pictures in the exhibition "Eight Dynasties of Chinese Painting" held at the Asia Society in 1981. "Arhats" and "bhikshus," Buddhist terms for individuals who have achieved various stages of enlightenment and are therefore venerated in the pictures.

Water, Heads, Hamptons
"To the white sands who will speak a name?" is derived from Hart Crane's line "To the white sand I may speak a name, fertile" in "O Carib Isle."

In The Mountains, Lines of Chinese Poetry
The epigraph is from "Wanderer's Song" by Meng Chiao, translated by A. C. Graham in *Poems of the Late T'ang*, p. 63.

Through The Binoculars
"Shambhala," the mythical kingdom referred to in Tibetan Buddhism whose inhabitants are all enlightened. The "story" told is one of the legends associated with the kingdom. "Are the cranes returning to you?" an anonymous line of Chinese poetry. "Of another poet . . ." refers to Wallace Stevens; "dangle down" are the last two words of his late poem, "Of Mere Being."

On Dry Lakes Trail
Dry Lakes Trail and Horn Peak are in the Sangre de Cristo mountains near Westcliffe, Colorado.

WORDFLOW: NEW AND SELECTED POEMS
(Talisman House Publishers, 1997)
Section "IV. NEW POEMS" contained previously uncollected poems.

Lecture With Celan
Italicized words are from *Paul Celan: Collected Prose*. Trans. Rosmarie Waldrop, (Carcanet, 1986).

Stanzas At Maresfield Gardens
Freud's residence, now a museum, is in Maresfield Gardens in Central London. The museum contains a replica of Freud's consulting room and houses many of the antiquities he collected. "*Adamah*" is Hebrew for 'ground' or 'earth' and is related to the name of Adam in the Old Testament.

Without Ozymandias
This poem is related to Shelley's "Ozymanias." Some of the imagery is from the landscape of the Great National Sand Dunes Monument in Southern Colorado, an area of nearly 100 square miles of rolling sand dunes resembling the interior of an African or Middle-Eastern desert. See also "Stanzas Without Ozymandias" and the note to that poem below.

In Paris

In 1996, terrorists set off bombs in the RER station under Boulevard St. Michel and on the Champs Elyseés. Goldenberg's restaurant was attacked by terrorists in 1982.

Prony's Calculations

Gaspard Clair François Marie Riche de Prony (1755 – 1839)—French mathematician and engineer. In 1793, de Prony began a major task of producing logarithmic and trigonometric tables, the *Cadastre*, viewed by the National Assembly as a monument to the science of the French Revolution.

Thinking of Mary

Mary Oppen (1908 – 1990), poet, translator, memorist and painter, wife of the poet George Oppen (1908 – 1984).

EXIGENT FUTURES: NEW AND SELECTED POEMS
(Salt Publishing Company, 2003).
"Section V, New Poems" contains previously uncollected work.

Cyclical

Divani Shamsi Tabriz (13th century Persian) was the son of an Imam and the friend and sometime mentor of Rumi (1207 – 1273).

"We can only wish valeat quantum valere potest."

The Latin proverb "valeat quantum valere potest" can be translated as "let it be valued according to its power." When my late friend, the poet Armand Schwerner, to whom this poem is dedicated, purchased his first fax machine, his initial transmission to me was a glossary of Sumero-Akkadian terms. The italicized words in the poem come from that glossary.

Winter Notes, East End

"Bardos" is plural for *bardo* which in Tibetan Buddhism is the intermediate state, lasting forty-nine days, between the individual's death and re-emergence into another life. "It is not possible to contract for a stay" a line from Schwerner's poem "the work," in *Selected Shorter Poems* (Junction Press, 1999) p. 97.

ESCHATON
(Talisman House Publishers, 2009)

Looking At Some Petroglyphs In A Dry Arroyo Near A Friend's House

The house referred to is the home of the poet Nathaniel Tarn. His wife, "Janet" of the poem, is Janet Rodney, a poet, printer and book maker. The arroyo runs behind their house in Tesuque, just north of Santa Fe, New Mexico.

On A Phrase Of Milosz's

Czeslaw Milosz (1911 – 2004), Polish poet and writer, Nobel Prize Laureate, 1980.

"Rilke's panther" refers to "The Panther" by Rilke. In Cid Corman's translation of the poem, the panther's gaze from his cage, enters the body and "stops being in the heart."

"Dark Talk"
The "muse" figure in the poem is loosely based on the late translator, anthologizer and scholar, Kathrine Washburn who in 2000 died of heart attack at the age of 57.

My City
Written after the attacks of September 11, 2001. The lines "The hole in the downtown/ sky" refers to the very visible gap left in the New York skyline by the fall of the World Trade Center towers.

Bandelette De Torah
The bandelette covers the exposed section of the Torah when it is unscrolled and lifted off the text when the text is being read. In Eastern Europe, the bandelette was called the Mappah. The *Yod* is used by the rabbi to point to the words being read as he intones from the Torah. *Davar* is the Hebrew word for both "word" and "thing." *Aleph,* the first letter of the Hebrew alphabet, is believed by kabbalists to be the primary instance of language, revelatory of all words and hence of all creation.

The Language Of The Jews
Gematria, a kabbalistic method of interpretation and divination, at once serious and playful, by which meaning is obtained through assigning numerical values to Hebrew letters.

Four London Windows
Westminster—written after a visit to Westminster Cathedral that happened to coincide with the anniversary of the death of T. S. Eliot. Blake's words can be found in *The Poetry and Prose of William Blake,* edited by David Erdman.

Horn Peak
Horn Peak, 13345 feet in height, dominates the Wet Mountain Valley, the area around Westcliffe, in southern Colorado.

Inflammation Of The Labyrinth
Dedicated to the poet and friend Harvey Shapiro (b. 1923). "The Red Wheelbarrow" refers William Carlos Williams's poem "The Red Wheel Barrow. In Orson Welles's film Citizen Kane, "Rosebud" is the last word uttered by the dying Charles Foster Kane, the word stenciled on the sled Kane used as a boy.

Homan's Etchings
Tiger Homan, Dutch painter and etcher, met at the Yaddo Art Colony in 1988. "*Anemos,*" *bosanemoon,*" and "*Tak Esdoorn,*" are the Dutch words for anemones and maple branch.

In The Studio
Dedicated to my friend Anthony Rudolf (b. 1942), poet, writer, translator and publisher of Menard Press. Rudolf has been a model for many figures in the pictures of Paula Rego, one of the major artists in Britain (see more on Rego below in the note to "The Assumption").

Poetic Geography
Dedicated to Rob Wilson (b. 1940), poet and scholar whose book *American Sublime* on the American landscape and the "nuclear sublime" inform this poem.

Report On The Dispatches
Throughout Operation Desert Storm, military briefings of the press were to news accuracy—to borrow from Tallyrand—what military music is to music. Many words (one thinks of terms such as "surgical strike" or "pinpoint bombing") had lost semantic significance as they were employed in massaging the psyches of reporters, and therefore of readers.

The Assumption
Paula Rego, (b. 1935), British painter of Portuguese descent. The picture on which the poem is based is one of a series on Biblical themes that Rego was commissioned to paint for the chapel of the Presidential Palace in Lisbon.

In Irons
The title is a sailing term. "In irons" describes the situation when the boat's prow is turned directly into the winds and the sail merely flaps, losing motive force, and the boat makes no headway.

A Terror Of Tonality
"*Zaum*"—the Russian Futurists' word signifying primordial speech, pre-rational and pre-semantic.

Stanzas Without Ozymandias
A re-write and re-conceptualization of "Without Ozymandias" p. 443 (see note to that poem above). The earlier version, though it had been anthologized and won an award, struck me as fragmentary, its disjunctive syntax problematic and exclusionary. In recasting the poem, I wanted to bring the fragments into, as Emerson termed it, "a meter-making argument," one that drew the reader into a symbolic realm cast by the words, to turn the poem from one of place to one of spiritual thought and its ramifications.

Eschaton
The title is from the Greek *oschatos/eschate*, meaning "concerning last things," especially the end of the world in Christian revelation. In some contexts, the word refers to a dramatic transformation of reality from what has been known or imagined.

Isohel
Isohel is a scientific term to describe an imaginary line on a map connecting places known to have equal durations of sunlight.

Ordinariness Of The Soul
The italicized first four lines are from the poetry of Lorine Niedecker. See "Along the river . . ." in *Lorine Niedecker: Collected Works*, p. 168.

An Interpellation
Interpellation is defined as the formal right of a parliment to submit questions to the government, i.e., to criticize the policies of a governing body, hence, also, an interruption into the way things are done.

At Work
"something they called pneumonia" and "a disease that finally had a name" refer to AIDs, which took a course for its victims from untreatable to treatable as it went from unnamable to unmentionable to discussable.

The Age Of The Poet
Rilke, in a letter to his Polish translator, asks whether one is able any longer to use words like "house," "home" or "tree."

Gloss
The epigraph is from Wallace Stevens's poem, "The House Was Quiet and The World Was Calm."

Ecologue
Hugh Seidman: see Note to the volume A LOOK AT THE DOOR WITH THE HINGES OFF.

Letter And Dream Of Walter Benjamin
All italicized words are from the writings of Benjamin.

The Visible
Port Bou is the seacoast border town in Spain where Walter Benjamin committed suicide in 1940. He is buried in the local cemetery.

Commentary Is The Concept Of Order For The Spiritual World
The title of the poem is from the writings of Gershom Scholem. The italicized words "*he is most apt,* etc . . ." are from the writings of Franz Rosenzweig (1889 – 1926), philosopher of Judaic thought and culture.

Mourning Field, Note Card
Reflections written in the immediate aftermath of September 11, 2001.

BECKMANN VARIATIONS & OTHER POEMS
(Shearsman Books, 2010).

"Beckmann Variations," the title work, is a mixed-genre, prose and poetry meditation focused on the life, paintings and writings of the German painter, Max Beckmann (1884 – 1950). One of the models for the work is W. B. Yeats's *Per Amica Silentia Lunae*, with its interweavings of prose passages and poetry. The study of *Per Amica* drew me back into Yeats's ruminations on power and violence, on theosophy, ruminations he shared with Beckmann. The more I studied Yeats, the more he seemed a likely guide or companion through which to view Beckmann's pictures. So while my speculations are primarily on Beckmann's art, they also invoke Yeats as a sort of Virgil figure to the moral, social and political infernos depicted in many of Beckmann's pictures. Titles of the poems are followed by the titles of the Beckmann pictures that suggested the poetry. The italicized last three lines of "Space" and the entire poem "Every So Often" are taken from Beckmann's writings.

Although only the poetry from the book is published here, a passage from the *Beckmann Variations* that relates to the poem "*Der Konig (The King), 1933, 1937)* is given below:

> Beckmann insisted that he hardly needed "to abstract things, for each object is unreal enough already, so unreal that I can make it real only by means of painting." Beckmann, laying out his designs, choosing the colors and their tints, composing in the manner of Yeats's vision of the "soul," and its "plastic power," a power that can "mould it to any shape it will by an act of imagination." Beckmann working in the style of the ancients who in their soul-making, Yeats said, "offered sheaves of corn, fragrant gums, and the odor of fruit and flowers, and the blood of victims."
>
> Both Beckmann and Yeats sensed the soul's inexpressibility, to be approached only by successive works, by catenaries of imaginings, unending works. Yeats exclaiming "because I seek an image not a book," that the wisest men in their writings were those "who own nothing but their blind stupefied hearts." He argued against "song," against sweetness or happiness, against the artist who became a "fly in marmalade." Underneath these thoughts is a fear, one that Beckmann shared, of being trapped by harmony and beauty, being lulled into easy belief, complacency or remorse. Beckmann endlessly instructs his students: " do not try to capture nature." Beckmann's longing can only be expressed in what cannot be a copied reality. His message to the poet is that nature is mute, inarticulate. The inexpressible produces words only as irritants, words that never leave off—one never quite arrives at the inexpressible.

The four poems on art subjects that were in the original volume are also included here.

Into The Heart Of The Real
The Sphinxes in Beckmann's painting are modeled on two sphinxes that sit atop the

gate posts of Wertheim Park, named for a Jewish philanthropist, in Amsterdam, the city Beckmann fled to the morning of July 19th, 1937 after hearing Hitler's speech the night before praising the opening that day of the Nazi exhibition, *Entartete Kunst* ("Degenerate Art"), held in Munich. Beckmann had by then been marked as a "degenerate artist," and his work was prominently displayed in the exhibition. In Amsterdam, shortly after the Nazi occupation, the Dutch collaborationist mayor of the city had the Wertheim name removed from the sphinx pillars. The German word *Abtransport* in Beckmann's title is the same word used to designate the deportation of the Jews of Germany and the Netherlands to the death camps.

Dead-ness
Although in many exhibitions, catalogs and writings on Beckmann's work, the title of the picture associated with this poem is given as "Death," Beckmann, in his own register of pictures entitled the painting "*Tot*," meaning "dead" and not "*Tod*," meaning "death."

Mother Asleep
The poem is based on a painting by the British artist Leon Kossoff (b.1926).

Notes: R. B. Kitaj At Marlborough
R. B. Kitaj (1932 – 2007), American-born painter, who spent much of his career in England and was associated with the School of London painters such as Frank Auerbach and Lucien Freud.

Within The Open Landscapes
The poem is based on a group of etchings and drawings by Jane Joseph, British artist.

Capriccio With Obelisk
The poem is based on pictures in the Bowes Museum in Barnard Castle, Durham County, England. The picture which gives the poem its title is "Architectural Capriccio With Obelisk" by the French painter Hubert Robert (1733 – 1808).

NEW POEMS

Anthrax In October
The anthrax scares that followed on September 11, 2011, enveloped New York and Washington in fear. The phrase "yellow submarines" refers to the Beatles' song line "we all live in a yellow submarine."

City, Matrix, Bird: Collage
This poem is the result of a collaborative effort with the painter BettyAnn Mocek for an exhibition created by Beth Shadur's Poetic Dialogue Project. The poem, constructed from a compilation and reworking of the many phrases in my poetry in which the word "bird" appeared, was mounted alongside Mocek's painting as the exhibition traveled around the United States in 2009.

Sangres Drought

George Oppen, American poet (1908 – 1984). "Sangres" is short for the Sangre de Cristo mountains. See note above for "With A Telescope In The Sangre De Cristos."

Deer And Voices On The Highway

Royal Gorge in Colorado, a spectacular natural canyon carved out by the Arkansas River, is spanned by the highest suspension bridge in the world, some nine hundred feet above the surface of the river. Tame deer wander peacefully along the road winding to the bridge.

After Baudelaire's Le Gouffre

"Le Gouffre," often translated as "The Abyss," with its implied critique of Pascal and other French thinkers, is thought to be one of Baudelaire's most 'philosophical' or 'anti-philosophical' poems.

For Carl

Written in honor of the hundredth birthday of the poet Carl Rakosi and originally published in postcard size as Mencard 142 by Anthony Rudolf's Menard Press in 2003. "Vee are lo-on-ely . . ." refers to William Carlos Williams's marvelous poem "Danse Russe" with its lines: "I am lonely, lonely/I was born to be lonely,/I am best so."

First Avenue

"MOSIACH," often translated as "Messiah." The dying rabbi of the poem was Rebe Menachem Mendel Schneerson, the Grand Rabbi of the Lubavitcher sect.

For Norman

Norman Finkelstein (b.1954), poet and scholar.

Afikomens

The title refers to the *afikomen*, the piece of matzoh broken off during the Passover Seder ceremony and hidden away for a child to find and receive a gift. The plural "afikomens" suggests attendance at many Seders, hence one's long life. The "New York City" section is a meditation on the city, post-9/11 (see also above, the poems, "My City," "Mourning Field, Note Card," "Anthrax In October," and "Now In The City"). Franz Rosenzweig (1886 – 929), an influential Jewish theologian and philosopher, and author of *The Star of Redemption*. "Hyponatremia" a life-threatening condition, often affecting atheletes such as marathon runners, where the ingestion of too much water dilutes the body's electrolytes, producing convulsions and coma. "Mon coeur mis a nu," the title of Baudelaire's prose journal, often translated as "My Heart Laid Bare."

Tibet: A Sequence

See author's note to the sequence. The series is based on Victor Segalen's *Odes suivies de Thibet* (Poesie/Gallimard, 1979). Segalen (1878 – 1919) was one of France's most remarkable writers. A medical doctor in the French Navy, he traveled extensively in Polynesia and the Far East, writing poetry, novels and ethnographic studies, including one of the first major works on "otherness" and Orientalism, *Essai sur L'Exotisme*. Epigraphs to sections of the sequence are modified translations from the notes in Segalen's *Odes*.

Animal Kingdom
"*mahakalas*"—tutelary deities, protectors of the teachings, often depicted in Tibetan thangkas as many-armed fierce creatures ringed with necklaces of skulls and surrounded by flames, their feet planted on the neck of a corpse representing the ego.

ACKNOWLEDGMENTS

I would like to thank the publishers of my previous books of poetry listed here for their support and encouragement: Coffee House Press: *In The Builded Place* (1989); Dos Madres Press: *A Look At The Door With The Hinges Off* (2006) and *Earth And Cave* (2006); Salt Publishers: *Exigent Futures: New and Selected Poems* (2003); Shearsman Books: *Beckmann Variations and other poems* (2010); Sumac Press: *Accidental Center* (1972); SUN: *Knowledge* (1979); Talisman House Publishers: *Wordflow: New and Selected Poems* (1997) and *Eschaton* (2009).

I am grateful to the editors and publishers in whose publications the poems in the "New Poems" section of this book, some slightly rewritten and with new titles, first appeared:

Big Bridge (online journal): "Anthrax In October" and "Maazel Conducts 'Arirang' in Pyongyang (26 Feb 2008)"

Collaborative Vision (catalog for The Poetic Dialogue Project exhibition): "City: Matrix: Bird: Collage"

Colorado Review: "Animal Kingdom," "Planetary Matters" and "Yak Blessing"

The Cultural Society (online journal): "Ready For Sunset," "Logobiography," "Loose Ode: Colorado," "Sentences," "Two-Tone Landscape," "Right After The Title Page," and "For Norman"

The Forward: "First Avenue"

Fresh Air: "Ode To The Sky On The Esplanade Of The New"

Golden Handcuffs: "Of The Limits"

Laurel Review: "Path"

Menard Press, as Mencards: "For Carl," in honor of the 100th birthday of Carl Rakosi, and "From The Notes" and "Kingdom's Winds," to celebrate the 70th birthday of Michael Heller

Poetry Salzburg Review: "After Baudelaire's *Le Gouffre*"

Shofar: "*Afikomens*"

Talisman: "The Form"

INDEX OF TITLES AND FIRST LINES

INDEX OF TITLES AND FIRST LINES . 573

ABOUT MICHAEL HELLER

Born in Brooklyn and raised in Miami Beach, Michael Heller was educated as an engineer at Rensselaer Polytechnic Institute. While working as a technical writer for Sperry Gyroscope, he met several former students of Louis Zukofsky, who introduced him to the work of a wide range of contemporary poets. In 1964 he won the New School's Coffey Poetry Prize and went abroad to continue to study and write. His poems first appeared in print in the nineteen sixties while he was living in a small village on Spain's Andalusian coast. In 1967, after returning to the United States, he took a position at New York University. Since then, he has published over twenty volumes of poetry, essays, memoir and fiction, including *Accidental Center* (1972), *In The Builded Place* (1979), *Wordflow* (1997), *Exigent Futures* (2003), *Living Root: A Memoir* (2000) and the prize-winning collection of essays, *Conviction's Net of Branches* (1985). Among his most recent works are a volume of poems, *Eschaton* (2009), a mixed genre work, *Beckmann Variations & other poems* (2010) and *Speaking the Estranged: Essays on the Work of George Oppen* (2008, expanded edition, 2012). Since the nineteen-nineties, he has been collaborating with the composer Ellen Fishman Johnson on multimedia works including the opera, *Constellations of Waking* (2000), based on the life of the German-Jewish writer Walter Benjamin, and the multimedia works, *This Art Burning* (2008) and *Out of Pure Sound* (2010), all of which premiered at the Philadelphia Fringe Festival. His writings on contemporary poetry, Judaic thought and on the intersections of Buddhist and Western philosophy and practice have appeared in various essay collections and journals. Among his many awards are grants and prizes from the Nation Endowment for the Humanities, the New York Foundation for the Arts, the Poetry Society of America and The Fund for Poetry. He resides in New York City and spends his summers in the Colorado mountains. He is married to the poet and scholar Jane Augustine.

NIGHTBOAT BOOKS

Nightboat Books, a nonprofit organization, seeks to develop audiences for writers whose work resists convention and transcends boundaries. We publish books rich with poignancy, intelligence, and risk. Please visit our website, nightboat.org, to learn about our titles and how you can support our future publications.

The following individuals have supported the publication of this book. We thank them for their generosity and commitment to the mission of Nightboat Books:

Kazim Ali
Anonymous
Elizabeth Motika
Benjamin Taylor

This book has been made possible, in part, by a grant from the New York State Council on the Arts Literature Program.

State of the Arts

NYSCA